Women's Studies and Studies of Women in Africa During the 1990s

Amina Mama

Working Paper Series 5/96

Women's Studies and Studies of Women
in Africa During the 1990s

© CODESRIA 1996

Typesetting : Sériane Camara

CODESRIA gratefully acknowledges the support of African Governments, the Swedish International Development Cooperation Agency (SIDA/SAREC), the International Development Research Centre (IDRC), the Ford Foundation, the Rockefeller Foundation, the Danish International Development Agency (DANIDA) and the Norwegian Ministry of Foreign Affairs.

The CODESRIA Working Paper Series is distributed free of charge to African research institutes and under the exchange programme of the CODESRIA Documentation Center (CODICE). Single copies can be obtained at US$8. For information, please contact :

      Publication Unit
      CODESRIA
      P.O. Box 3304
      Dakar, Senegal.

Table of Contents

The Author V
Acknowledgement VII
Abstract 1
Introduction 2
Women, Politics, and the State 11
    Pre-colonial States 11
    Colonial States 12
    National Liberation 15
    Post-independence States 16
Cultural Studies 27
    Ideologies of Domesticity 28
    Women, Religion, Resistance 29
    Sexuality 39
        Imperial Sexuality 39
        The Nation and the Family 41
        Genital Mutilation 43
    Herstories: Giving Voice to Women 48
Work and Economy 55
    Conceptual Issues 55
    Women's Work in Precolonial Africa 57
    Labour Relations during Colonialism 60
        Women and Waged Work in Colonial Africa 61
        Colonial Informal Sector 66
    Contemporary Situation 69
        The Formal Sector 70
        The Informal Sector Post-Independence 74
        Sex Work 78
Conclusions: Whither African Women's Studies? 81
Bibliography 85

The Author

Amina Mama is a Nigerian scholar, and the author of *Beyond the Masks: Race, Gender and Subjectivity* (Routledge 1995), *The Hidden Struggle: Statutory v Voluntary Sector Responses to Violence Against Black Women* (London 1989). She holds a doctorate in applied psychology, has taught at a number of European and international institutions.

Acknowledgements

My thanks to Chairmaine Pereira, Kate Meagher and Yahaya Hashim of the centre for Research and Documentation in Kano, and to Pepe Roberts of the University of Liverpool, for their constructive comments on an early draft of this paper. I also wish to acknowledge the assistance of the library staff of the Institute for Development Studies at the University of Sussex, James Currey of James Currey Ltd, Sarah LaRose of New Beacon Books, and Camilla Patel of Lynne Rienner publications, London Office.

Abstract

The publication of the CODESRIA Green Book *Women's Studies and Studies of Women in Africa During the 1990's* comes at a time of upsurge in gender and women's studies across Africa. Amina Mama, has written a document which covers three main areas of the literature in what has become a vast field of research, teaching and activism in and beyond Africa. Following an introduction which situates African women's studies in the context of international feminism, regional political and institutional conditions, the first section addresses recent publications in the general field of state and politics, from precolonial times to the present. Section two reviews a range of material grouped under the heading of cultural studies: namely studies of women and gender dynamics in the areas of religion and sexuality, and the innovative women-speak research favoured by the women's movement, often referred to as 'Herstories'. Section three is devoted to a consideration of the historical and contemporary literature on all aspects of women's involvement in various spheres of work and the economy. To conclude, the author questions the relationship between women's studies and the women's movement in Africa, highlighting the importance of developing and activist intellectual tradition in which African women's studies emanate from the concerns of interests of the African women's movement, and are directed towards the positive transformation of African gender relations.

Introduction

The almost worldwide emergence of women's studies as a field of research, teaching and study is generally viewed as resulting from the impact of the international women's movement on the academic establishment. Over ten years after the United Nations Decade for Women held its final conference in Nairobi, the year after the Beijing Conference seems an appropriate time for us to review the contribution of women's studies and gender research to social science in and on Africa.

Publications in these areas have proliferated, testifying to the opening up of a vast new field of research, and to the generation of a new body of knowledge that is not only about women, but largely carried out by women scholars motivated by their expressed commitment to furthering the interests of women. While there have always been studies of women, the women's studies that emerged in the 1970s and 1980s was almost exclusively research and teaching conducted 'on women, by women, for women' that is to say, it was firmly identified with the feminist agenda of liberating women. Such studies can justifiably be referred to as 'feminist studies', because they had a progressive political agenda as well as an intellectual one. During the 1970s feminists in the West, determined not only to gain a place in these bastions of male privilege and power, but also to transform them into places where women too could study, develop and empower themselves, mounted a full scale assault on the academies. This assault took various forms.

Some women sought the establishment of certified courses in women's studies in the existing institutions of formal education. Others concentrated their efforts on fighting for better representation of women in the mainstream of the academic establishment, arguing that more women should be appointed to the staff and administration of higher education institutions, and that more female students should be admitted to hitherto male-dominated areas of study. Yet other women, disaffected by the existing systems, pioneered the establishment of independent study groups, libraries, research and documentation centres for women. Feminists engaged in science have made major theoretical and methodological contributions to world scholarship across the disciplines. It is now possible to speak confidently of 'feminist science' and debate the ideas of feminist philosophy and epistemology, feminist theory, feminism and methodology, and feminist research, and to refer to the extensive literature on all of these. It is also possible to identify feminist contributions to any of the major disciplines.

Women's studies, defined by their historical link to the women's movement, have thus given birth to a range of changes within the scientific academies, and within scientific production. The extent of the link between the women's movement and academic feminism has become a subject for debate, both in the West and in the rest of the world. The term 'feminist studies' has been coined by those concerned to emphasize the link between activism and intellectualism in the service of women's liberation. Others have opted to use the more neutral and inclusive term 'gender studies' instead of either women's or feminist studies, ostensibly to convey greater neutrality, and to turn the lens on the oppressors (men) as well as on the oppressed (women), or 'gender analysis' to denote social analysis that is premised on recognition of gender inequality.

The extent to which these paradigmatic changes have penetrated African studies and African social science is difficult to ascertain. Some light can be cast on the question by considering that rather diffuse area of research that can only loosely be gathered under the heading of African women's studies. For pragmatic reasons, in what follows, women's studies is defined inclusively as studies of women, studies by women, and studies for women, rather than limiting consideration to studies which are all three of these. This is because the link to the women's movement is no longer as clear and concise as historians of women's studies in Europe and North America would have us believe it used to be. More pertinently, there are good grounds for supposing that African women's studies are undergoing their own distinct evolution.

Women's studies have emerged more recently in Africa, with significant numbers of African women really only developing interest in the 1980s. Prior to this virtually all studies of African women were carried out by Western researchers on anthropological forays into the largely untouched territory of African women's lives (Paulme 1963, Rosaldo and Lamphere 1974, reviews by Wipper 1972, 1988). The earliest anthropological studies were purportedly apolitical rather than feminist, but since the 1970s, anthropological studies of African women have increasingly been influenced by the concerns of the women's movement. Nonetheless, it is clear that they have remained studies of 'Other' women, if not studies of 'woman as Other' (de Beauvoir 1972).

In the middle of the 1990s it is important to assess the extent to which this legacy has persisted: to what extent can we say that women's studies carried out in Africa now emanate from African as opposed to external and Western interests and forces? If we decide that the answer to this question varies from one place to another, then we might put the question another way and ask. what are the conditions which bestow distinctive characteristics on African women's studies? We can no longer disregard the local and regional influences on this growing body of thought. Today growing numbers of African scholars of both sexes are involved in studies of women and gender relations, carrying out work far removed from the early feminist anthropological studies of women. However, the extent to which these are merely studies of women, as proposed to feminist studies deserves some attention.

Although we can link the genesis of women's studies in Africa to the rise of the women's movement internationally, it would be fallacious to insist that African women's studies are generated exclusively by regional or national women's movements. Other factors are clearly at play. Amongst these are the influence of the development industry, national and subregional political conditions, the crisis in African education and the emergence of state feminism. All of these make it pertinent to ask whether African women's studies can be said to have emerged in the service of African feminism in the same way that say North American or European women's studies are said to have emerged as the intellectual wing of a more widespread women's movement[1] So, what kind of linkage can be traced between African feminism and African women's studies? Very often it seems that this potentially transformational field of study runs the risk of being reduced to an expedience deployed by undemocratic regimes seeking legitimacy, or a donor-driven phenomenon irrelevant to the democratisation process. This in turn leads us to pose a strategic question: what can be done to strengthen the links that do exist between African women's studies and the African women's movement, and so to ensure that African women's studies emanate from the collective concerns and interests of African women?

---

1   Even in the West, there is a lively debate on the relationship between the women's liberation movement and women's studies, the latter constantly being accuses of being deradicalised into an 'academic feminism' that has ceased to have practical application. (Currie and Kazi 1987). Others have protested against the 'bureacratisation' of feminism (Mueller 1986).

The reticence of the African middle class towards the idea of women's liberation has meant that only an intellectual minority of this class have overtly embraced feminism, articulating the oppressed situation of African women in political terms. For the most part the African intelligentsia has preferred to dismiss feminism as something alien and Western, to regard the international women's movement as resulting from the activities of a covey of sexually abnormal, man-hating eccentrics far removed from the concerns of 'real' African women. The 'real' African woman of the collective imagination is content with her subordinate position as wife, mother and beast of burden. She is passive in the face of abuse, tolerant of all forms of infidelity; her only real ambition is to retain respectability by labouring for the maintenance of a stable marriage and family and seeing to the satisfaction of her husband's desires (see e.g. Babangida 1988).

Concern over the marginalisation of women in African societies only really took firm root in the consciousness of Africans when the decade for women ushered in a discourse which did not challenge the gross inequalities of prevailing gender relations, under the rubric of 'women in development'. WID, as it became known is able to avoid directly challenging patriarchy and capitalism and demanding the confrontation of women's oppression, instead targeting women as a group to be 'integrated into development'. Under this rubric, governments of whatever political colour are called upon to mobilize women for their vaguely defined development agenda, in the name of the equally vague notion of national interest. This call gave rise to the establishment of regional and national governmental machineries for women all over the region, ranging from women's desks in ministries of social welfare, to departments of women's affairs, to the grandly named ministries for women and development. Indeed many of these high-profile structures were pioneered in Africa, and became a source of regional pride (Snyder and Tadesse 1995). However, so far there is little evidence that government structures for women have become effective vehicles for the articulation and defense of women's collective concerns and interests.

In contrast to the conservative tone of women in development (WID) discourses, the long involvement of women in the radical politics of the region has given rise to a more subversive tradition of militancy with clearly feminist elements. As early as the 1920s, Egyptian women in the nationalist movement had formed an autonomous organisation, the Egyptian Feminist Union, and were producing their own magazine (*L'Egyptienne* founded in 1925). However, it was more typical for women to throw their support behind male-led struggles than to organize autonomously to fight for more equal gender relations. During the 1950s Ghanaian women rallied around Nkrumah's calls for mass mobilization, and Kenyan women took to the bush as fighters and played key roles in support of the Land and Freedom Army. During the 1960s Algerian women joined the National Liberation Front (FLN) to smuggle weapons and explosives and carry out intelligence work against the French, Josina Machel formed the first women's unit in the FRELIMO guerrilla force and Angolan women responded to Augustino Neto's call to resist the Portuguese, to name only a few of the examples enriching African history. Women's involvement in African liberation struggles became a favoured subject for feminist scholars during the 1970s and 1980s, hence the documentation of numerous historical examples of female militancy across the region, not so much amongst the elite as amongst ordinary women in both rural and urban communities (Amadiume 1987, Urdang 1989, Walker 1991, Manuh 1991a).

During the 1970s, the domination of international fora by Western women with at best charitable attitudes to women from the capitalist periphery increasingly came under challenge. A small number of highly educated African women entered the fray, protesting against their being marginalised, and demanding that their voice be heard. At the intellectual level, it was made clear that African women were no longer content to merely be the objects of study, whose situation was used to test and verify theories conceptualised elsewhere, by Western women scholars whose concerns and preoccupations often differed from their own.

With the establishment of the Association of African Women for Research and Development (AAWORD) in 1977, African feminist intellectuals sought to institutionalize their presence, and so to articulate the agenda of African feminism by facilitating research and activism by African women scholars. Early in its existence AAWORD facilitated workshops on methodology, women and rural development, reproduction, the mass media and development assistance. Despite these promising beginnings, and for reasons that cannot be detailed here, AAWORD has so far not been very successful in achieving its goals, or in bringing together the growing numbers of African women scholars now involved in women's studies and gender research within and beyond the region.

In the absence of a viable regional forum however, a series of nationally-based initiatives have given autonomous voice to African women scholars, amongst these the Women's Research and Documentation Centre at Ibadan University, the Development and Women's Studies group at the University of Ghana, the Women's Research and Documentation Project at the University of Dar-es-Salaam, the gender unit at Eduardo Mondlane University in Mozambique, and several others in the process of formation. A number of primarily activist projects have also generated new understandings of women's realities, among these the Zimbabwe Women's Resource Centre Network, Women in Nigeria, the Tanzanian Media Women's Association, and Zambian women working on woman abuse. There has also been a proliferation of regional and subregional projects and networks working on gender issues, of which the Women and Law in Southern Africa project has perhaps been the most dynamic to date. A number of university courses have also been established over the years, but a great many of these have remained under-staffed, under-resourced and marginal, often depending on the efforts of individual faculty members and a high degree of voluntarism (e.g. those at Ahmadu Bello University in Zaria, Nigeria, Makerere in Uganda, and at the Universities of Addis Ababa, Zimbabwe and most recently, Malawi).

In keeping with this situation, it is true to say that most of the material published within the region has not been generated within any autonomous African feminist forum. Instead, most of it has been either undertaken by scholars visiting from more affluent places, or by individual African scholars, often operating under extremely difficult conditions. Some work under the auspices of national universities, but have to rely on international donors for financial support. Others are only able to carry out research in unequal collaboration with Western scholars who are able to bring in the funds. A great many other would-be-researchers have no access to research funds, and are obliged to find other ways of earning their daily bread. The most foolhardy embark on unsponsored research, and if they do manage to produce research reports, these then lie undeveloped and gathering dust on office shelves, never making it into published form.

It seems fair to say that although African women have long been favoured as objects of study, it is taking a long time for African women's studies studies by African women and/or for African women to develop. Combined with the dismal decline of African universities over the last two decades, it has been difficult to sustain the material base of the research community and its intellectual autonomy, let alone open up new areas of study (see Diouf and Mamdani 1994).

CODESRIA's 1991 seminar on Gender Analysis was the first regional gathering to include both men, who treated the issues with varying degrees of seriousness, and women (see Imam, Mama and Sow forthcoming). Heated debates culminated in participants achieving some consensus that gender research was a legitimate enterprise to engage in, and one which had already yielded a body of knowledge and methodological innovations of value to African social science in general (El-Bakri and Besha 1989, Meena 1992).

Isolated examples like these notwithstanding, it is still true to say that a disproportionate amount of the internationally available research on African women and African gender relations is carried out by Western scholars, often guided by philosophical, theoretical and methodological concerns that emanate from Western rather than African feminism. This is particularly evident when we consider the publication lists of the major international publishing houses. It is significantly less evident from the listings of in-house research and publications produced in local research institutions and universities for here we see that there is a burgeoning interest in women's studies that is being spearheaded by African women scholars. All over the region, African women have pushed for the introduction of courses in women's studies, and for the establishment of units, programmes and departments to facilitate the development of both teaching and research. While some have pursued women's studies in its own right, others have settled for the wider and more acceptable rubric of gender studies, or directed their efforts towards inclusion of gender issues in the academic mainstream (Musoke 1992, African Studies Association 1991). The push for institutionalization of women's and gender studies is remarkable in view of the impoverished and declining condition of so many African academic institutions.

The following essay considers women's studies research conducted in and on Africa during the last six years, regardless of the race or origin of the individual scholars. Needless to say one cannot help being cognizant of the fact that unequal power relations exist between Western and African scholars, as much within women's studies as elsewhere. African women scholars have a resentment of this situation that is healthy only insofar as it inspires them to produce more and better quality work. It is a resentment that is counterproductive when used as an excuse for intellectual tardiness and sloppy production. There is a tendency amongst African scholars to react against the evident hegemony of Western academics, and to ignore the very high quality work that some of the Western and white African scholars are producing. In the field of women's studies, much of the recent work is both intellectually rigorous and politically more correct than the early studies which provoked the ire of black and African scholars in the 1980s (Carby 1982, Amos and Parmar 1984, Mohanty 1988). Within the field of women's studies in and on Africa, it would be dishonest to deny the fact that some white women have indeed listened, taking on the critiques of black feminists to advance theoretically and politically (Carby 1982). Furthermore, amongst African scholars, the black feminist critique of imperialistic and racist elements within Western feminism is often misunderstood, and taken as grounds for a cavalier indictment and rejection of all and any form of 'feminism'. As a result much that is of great value within feminist scholarship is ignored, and the high quality of some of the most impressive work on and about African women and gender relations is denied, simply because it has been carried out by foreigners.

The aim of this review is to stimulate and inspire the production of more and higher quality work in the field of African women's studies. In so doing I assume that encouraging more African scholars to undertake and engage in research and publication in this area is the best way of doing this. Not only can indigenous scholars bring local understanding of the subtleties and nuances of our diverse and rapidly changing realities to bear in theorising and knowledge production, but the possibilities of conducting academic work with intrinsic value to the communities under study are far greater if such scholarship is indigenously grounded. No doubt anthropology has generated a great many insights into so-called primitive societies; even so, the achievements of anthropologists are seldom compared to those of Marx or Freud or Foucault all of whom have developed their theory in reference to a detailed understanding of the societies they knew best. When Africans study Africa, not only are the conclusions they draw about African societies often different from those reached by others, as Diop's historiography or Hountoundji's philosophy indicate, but their theoretical and philosophical relevance to the region and to world scholarship is likely to be more profound (e.g. Diop 1974; Hountoundji 1983).

In discussing the rather wide-ranging selection of material gathered for this review, I concentrate on drawing out the main preoccupations and theoretical advances in each area of interest. In the final section I examine the extent to which women's studies in Africa successfully reflect the African feminist agenda of transforming gender relations in the direction of greater equity.

While I initially made a distinction between gender and women's studies, the literature searches revealed that the vast majority of 'gender studies' in and on Africa were in fact 'women's studies' insofar as it was hard to find any studies of men, masculinity or male power per se. In short, in Africa at least, gender studies are still women's studies. While I do refer to work on gender relations specifically, I have not included mainstream work that shows itself to be aware of gender. Many such studies included a few references to women or 'the woman question', or even of women's oppression, but these did not warrant special consideration: it is what one would expect to happen in the context of a global spread and growth of feminist ideas.

My initial literature searches revealed a vast number of publications released over the last five years. A significant proportion of these are reports produced by international agencies and aid organisations, notably the International Bank for Reconstruction and Development (IBRD) better known as the World Bank, the various United Nations agencies and other multilateral and bilateral agencies. These I have not included in this review. Instead I have limited my consideration to publications from universities, research organisations and those non governmental agencies involved primarily in research (like the Centre for Basic Research in Uganda, the Organisation for Social Science Research in East Africa (OSSREA), the Council for the Development of Social Science Research in Africa and the Association of African Women for Research and Development (AAWORD). My coverage is thematic rather than comprehensive, and is confined to materials published in English. I leave to others the task of carrying out similar studies of French, Portuguese and Arabic language publications in this wide and changing field.

To make discussion coherent, I have found it expedient to group the material into a number of areas. This does not mean that these areas are distinct. For example it is apparent that many publications concerned with sexuality could be grouped readily under the heading of health and reproduction or under cultural studies. Sex work could come under sexuality, but I chose to place it under work since the most insightful research on the subject looked at it as an economic activity. Where the discussion demands, items are referred to under more than one heading. The three major divisions I finally decided to use are as follows:

Women and the State: to include governance, politics, nationalism, liberation movements and structures for women.

Culture: religion, sexuality, identity and life history studies.

Work and economy: urban and rural, formal and informal sectors, domestic labour and sex work.

Each section comprises a discussion of the literature reviewed in the light of the concerns raised by way of introduction. This is intended both to indicate the state of the art and to identify areas for further work, particularly by scholars based within the African region.

I conclude with a brief consideration of the future of African gender and women's studies in the region and the implications for African feminism.

Women, Politics, and the State
Pre-colonial States

Very few historical studies of the role of African women in pre-colonial African states appear to have been conducted over the last five years. This has helped to perpetuate the general paucity of information and understanding of gender relations and women's lives in that period. Even prior to this, information has been often been as much mythological as factual. Nonetheless the cultural and psychological importance of well-known historical figures like 16th century Amina of Zazzau and the 18th century Nzinga of Angola, is evident in the evolving feminist consciousness of African women. Awareness of this must lie behind the publication of accessible collections of profiles of eminent women in history for school or university use (e.g. Sweetman 1984, Awe 1992).

A number of earlier studies emphasized the complementarity of sex roles in what they describe as 'dual-sex systems' of government. This thesis put forth the argument that the European colonial state excluded African women from playing hitherto important and valued roles in political life (e.g. Okonjo 1983, Arhin 1983, Amadiume 1987), a thesis which must be viewed more critically today in the light of the evidence that in pre-colonial systems too, most women were subordinate to most men (Manuh 1991a).

Musisi (1991) provides us with a rare study of the relationship between women, polygyny and the state in pre-colonial Buganda. She confronts the methodological challenge of relying on limited information, undertaking a reinterpretation of the available accounts, both ethnographic and biographical, written by men. These, she supplements with interviews with 'the last wife of nineteenth century royalty'. Her study reveals how political structures both shape and are shaped by the marital and gender relations of the ruling class, particularly by the 'grand polygyny' practised by the political elite. State formation coincided with increased social inequality, and a deterioration in women's power was one aspect of this. Nonetheless, her research demonstrates the involvement of Buganda women in state formation, not only as mothers of kings and king-makers, but also as providers of political balance and cementers of alliances. While very few women wielded much real power (notably princesses, who were also exempted from marriage), a great many functioned as objects of exchange in relationships between men and groups of men. This study indicates not only how much can be learned from studies of how pre-colonial gender relations affected and were affected by politics and statecraft, but that the method of reanalyzing existing data from a gendered perspective is a viable one which can open up this neglected area of historiography (see also Mikell's 1989 paper on the role of women in the Akan kingdoms).

Even the most recent publications on ancient and pre-colonial Africa supply little detailed information on the roles of non-royal women in politics and statecraft. Because of the focus on the few exceptionally powerful women who have invariably been members of the feudal aristocracies, one might be forgiven for gaining the impression that ordinary women in general were politically unimportant in many African societies. However, earlier historical studies suggest that no such conclusion is warranted in the absence of further empirical research on the subject (Leith-Ross 1939, Okonjo 1983).

Colonial States

Studies of the colonial period are far more numerous. Much of this work initially set out to counter the imperialist claim that colonialism improved the condition of African women, hitherto living as slaves and beasts of burden at the mercy of virulently patriarchal traditional cultures. What has been revealed is a far more complex scenario, in which transformations in gender relations have not only been mediated by class, ethnic and cultural factors, but have also varied widely across Africa and between different forms and stages of colonialism. Colonial states appear not to have ever resolved the administrative, legal and social problems posed by the fact that whereas the state required certain things of men and set about exploiting and extracting these, African societies have always comprised both men and women. The resulting confusion is reflected in the contradictory official attitudes towards the presence of women, particularly apparent in the administration of urban areas. Here we see that periods of tolerance, during which women settled in the towns performing various tasks which usefully provided all manner of social services to men recruited to live and work in labour compounds, have been interrupted by the harsh imposition of decrees and edicts designed to remove women from the towns (White 1990, Schmidt 1991, Barnes 1992). Clean-up campaigns sought to selectively remove women viewed as disreputable, explicitly those engaged in liquor brewing and selling and the provision of sexual services. Yet, the virtual absence of social and welfare provisions meant that removing even targeted groups of women also undermined the informal systems that sustained the cheap labour pool on which the colonial state relied.

Writing on Zimbabwe (then Southern Rhodesia) Schmidt (1991) uses detailed evidence to argue that there was deliberate connivance between African patriarchs who felt that women were 'getting out of control' and colonial authorities for whom the control of women's and children's labour by African men was necessary for both the establishment and the consolidation of colonial rule. What is clear is that African and European men shared the idea that African women were inferior beings who should be kept under male control. Consequently, both were disturbed by the growing tendency of women to exercise greater mobility and to flee the tyranny and drudgery of life in the homesteads, something that is clearly reflected in the numerous recorded complaints to the authorities between 1910 and the 1930's. In her book, Schmidt (1991:734) details various ways in which inflexible customary laws were developed so as to coerce women into staying with their husbands, highlighting the way in which indigenous and European structures of patriarchal control reinforced and transformed one another, evolving into new structures and forms of domination.

Barnes (1992) takes a slightly different position, emphasizing the ambivalence of a colonial state which provided few services for the indigenous workforce, and therefore ultimately relied on the services provided by African women in the towns and mine compounds. Although she is reluctant to support Schmidt's (1991) thesis of an 'unholy alliance' between patriarchies, Barnes (1992) too draws our attention to the disapproval of women's mobility and the 'immorality' that both African and European men associated with their presence. The contradictory policies that were deployed in colonial efforts to allow some categories of women and yet remove others from urban areas reflected a deeper struggle over the appropriation of women's labour.

Literature on this period highlights the way in which the colonial era, accompanied by the introduction and consolidation of capitalism, saw a gradual commodification of gender relations. The tradition of lobola for example, changed from being symbolic to becoming an important source of cash which men could rely upon to pay taxes and other expenses. This was the case until their daughters started moving to the towns and selling their services directly to men, keeping the money themselves. Documenting the shifts in policy over time, Barnes (1992) concludes that in this contradictory policy climate, the constant resourcefulness of women produced an administratively insoluble situation. In the end, a great many women retained their mobility, thereby gaining some control over the fruits of their labour under hostile circumstances.

Studies of the actual role of women in colonial government have until recently been rare. Denzer (1989) provides us with a study of women's employment in colonial government service, in Nigeria between 1862-1945. Here women were largely deprived of access to education, something she attributes to the fact that 'Nigerian and British attitudes concerning female roles had much in common' (1989:6). Once women did start formal schooling, there was a slow incorporation of women into very restricted areas of government service — women could only be employed in the positions of nurse, lady physician, school mistress, education superintendent or confidential secretary. Even in these select areas, women were denied access to any position requiring them to exercise authority over men, a policy justified on the basis that the idea would be too alien to Africans. So began the institutionalised gender segregation that has affected the employment of women in government — the largest formal employer — to date. Even the nursing profession was dominated by Nigerian men until 1949, when a policy to replace them with more women was introduced. Denzer catalogues the pioneering careers of the individual women who did work in government during the colonial period.

Both Manuh (1991) and Perbi (1992) reveal a similar pattern of gender segregation in colonial Ghana, with even the most highly qualified women being refused entry to the administrative class of civil servants, and those employed being expected to resign once they married or got pregnant.

Similar studies pulling out the available data in a range of African countries would be of great benefit to our analyses and understanding of the gender dynamics pervading contemporary African states, and highlighting some of the long-standing obstacles to women's equal participation in governance today.

National Liberation

Studies of women's participation in national liberation and independence movements have been more numerous than those of women in colonial states. One wonders if this reflects the identification of feminism with other liberation movements? If early studies were optimistic about the potential for the transformation of gender relations through women's involvement in national liberation struggles (Urdang 1979, Mies and Reddock 1982), research conducted in the 1980's has more often reflected disappointment that the fruits of liberation appear not to have been equally shared between the genders; Algeria and Zimbabwe being the most obvious examples.

In the last six years these have been only slightly tempered by more mature assessments of how far the exigencies of war can be expected to translate into women's equality once the war is over, and other forms of subversion take over (e.g. Urdang 1989, Lazreg 1990, 1994). Incisive analyses of the gender politics of women's participation in either the army or the armed struggle dispense with the notion that picture-poster images of women carrying guns herald women's liberation (Cock 1992). History has taught us that participation in armed struggle does not guarantee gender equality in peacetime, with commentators on Zimbabwe drawing our attention to the harassment and humiliations experienced by former freedom fighters disparaged on the basis they are said not to make 'good wives'.

Urdang's (1989) study of post-independence Mozambique catalogues the way in which post-war reconstruction and development were being hampered by South African-backed sabotage. Here, economic catastrophe has followed the war and undermined the struggle for change. These generally unfavourable factors notwithstanding, she also discusses the loss of momentum with regard to women's liberation, specifically noting a number of opportunities missed by the official Organisation of Mozambican Women (OMM). Never an autonomous movement, the OMM appears to have offered rearguard support for the ruling party and concentrated its efforts on mobilizing women for political support and economic production, that is, in rather less than revolutionary areas. From her account, even the famous Frelimo Women's Detachment founded by Josina Machel in the 1960s appears to have been more of a ploy to shame men into fighting than anything else, given that women who joined up were deployed not as combat troops, but rather as porters, caterers and providers of other support services (Urdang 1989). With apartheid South Africa supporting RENAMO during the period of her research, actual transformation of gender relations was clearly being subsumed in the struggle to survive, with the heady promises and commitments to the liberation of women which were made in the earlier period remaining unfulfilled.

Lazreg's analysis of gender and politics in colonial Algeria (1990) notes that the French had an obsessive preoccupation with Islam. In popular reactions against this, Islamic conservativism became a key aspect of Algerian self-identity. Similarly, the repeated attempts of the French to symbolically appropriate Algerian women (e.g. by unveiling them on public stages) alongside their appropriation of the Algerian nation, had persistent undermining effects on Algerian gender politics, effects only partly mitigated by the heroism that women demonstrated during the war. Even then the FLN's definition of women's tasks was based on the conventional sexual division of labour, allocating to women the tasks of lending support to combatants (male), information, liaison and supply work, sheltering militants from the police and assisting the families of guerrillas and prisoners (Lazreg 1990, 1994 Tlemcani 1992). Nonetheless, as these writers point out, even this somewhat limited participation in the war marked such a radical break with tradition, that it has not been without influence in post-independence politics.

Post Independence States

I have noted elsewhere that the constitutional and legal status of women and the level of women's participation in governance are often taken as key indicators of the general level of democracy in a society (Mama 1995a). Because of the history of women's involvement in the independence struggle waged across the region, in Africa it is also taken as a measure of the extent to which the promises of nationalism have been fulfilled. Since the UN Decade for Women (1975-1985) and the rise of a highly articulate international women's movement, governments everywhere have found it expedient to display a certain level of commitment to the participation of women in development. International donor insistence that attention be given to 'the gender question' has now been incorporated into the post-Cold-War preoccupation with democratisation. It is in this context that African governments have lately come under international pressure to become more democratic. Under the twin rubrics of 'multipartyism' and 'good governance' international bureaucracies have now begun to articulate their disillusionment with military dictatorships, one-party states and the other male-dominated forms of authoritarianism which they have for so long financed and supported. Whatever rhetoric is used, women's involvement in politics and governance is rightly seen as integral to democratisation. Furthermore, a decade after hosting the Nairobi conference, African women themselves now expect to play more significant roles in national politics and public life.

In view of the patriarchal character of colonialism itself, and the correspondingly high level of women's participation in independence struggles, it is somewhat ironic that post-independence governments have not made more viable efforts to involve women at decision-making levels of politics, finance and governance. Instead, we have a situation in which wealthy Western nations, now operating as creditors instead of colonial powers, and formerly so disinterested in the well-being of African women, are one of the main forces pushing African governments to address themselves to the question of improving women's level of participation. Indeed, the empirical evidence shows that the vast majority of African women are still working like beasts of burden in under-renumerated tasks, still almost completely excluded from decision-making levels of government, and playing only marginal roles in national politics and public life.

Perhaps it is because women are so marginally involved in government in Africa that scholars have been slow to examine the gender dynamics in statecraft and politics. Yet it is precisely in the areas of government, statecraft and politics that, at least until recently, the bulk of national resources and decision-making power have been concentrated, and from which women have been largely excluded.

The research that has been carried out on the subject of women and the state in Africa has not taken women as actors within the state, or looked at their participation in the public services, administration or policy-making. The influential collection edited by Parpart and Staudt (1989) primarily addresses the effects of the colonial and post-colonial state on different aspects of women's lives, lives which are portrayed as being lived largely outside the auspices of government and the formal economy. It is generally agreed that the state has acted primarily as a vehicle for elite male interests, enhancing and extending men's power over women and offering women little access to ownership of land or means of production, few avenues for participation in the formal economy, and even less political power. Some researchers have drawn attention to the means by which women have struggled to defend and advance their collective and individual interests under changing conditions (Mbilinyi 1989, Munachonga 1989, Hansen 1992, Jacobs 1989, Tsikata 1990, Schmidt 1991, Barnes 1992). Nonetheless, Chazan (1989:186) feels able to conclude that African women have played no significant role in statecraft, and have not been able to influence decision-makers in any consistent manner. She feels that this is why state policies towards them have continued to be both discriminatory and coercive. Whether or not one agrees with the grim conclusion that Chazan was able to draw at the end of the 1980s, it is still worth asking whether the same conclusion could be drawn today?

The early emphasis on the effects of the state on women generated little discussion of women's overt or covert influence on national politics and policy-making. This may partly be because the state itself has been conceptualised in fairly monolithic terms until as recently as the late 1980s. The model of the African state is that of a powerful leviathan acting on the various groups within society. With a strongly dominant central state in operation, marginalised social groups experience the state as oppressive and exploitative, rather than beneficial. Since the state does not serve their interests, many choose to operate largely outside the realm of the state, a notion encapsulated in the concept of 'exit' (Fatton 1989).

More recent work by African feminist scholars has overturned the notion that women exist largely outside the state, beginning to analyze women's role in statecraft itself (Tsikata 1989, Manuh 1993, Mama 1995a). Generally these studies examine the important roles that women and their organisations have played in support of nationalist movements and political parties, but bemoan their lack of success in effecting changes in gender politics and advancing women's interests. Tsikata's study targets women's political organisations in Ghana, providing us with a critical and clear sighted analysis of how it is that, despite the impressively high level of activity, these have not been able to tackle the important problems faced by women in Ghana. This failure is attributed to:

> the unfavourable political climate for independent struggles; the political character and practice of the organizations in question; and weaknesses arising from the lack of a tradition of independent political organization in the country (Tsikata 1989:73-74)

Tsikata documents a pattern of co-option of women's organisations by the ruling groups — first by Nkrumah's Convention People's Party and more recently by the Provisional National Defence Council under Rawlings.

She concludes that for women's political organizations to outlive the ruling regime, and to be more effective vehicles for women's political as well as social interests, would require a change in the political culture. Such a change would favour independent organisation and the pursuit of objectives emanating from the concrete conditions of ordinary women's lives, rather than objectives thought up by a leadership representing ruling political interests.

Manuh (1993) also writing about Ghana, analyses relations between women, society and the state under the rule of the PNDC. She comes to similar conclusions regarding the need for greater independence of women's organisation. In fact, Manuh's analysis of the women's movement concludes that this has not so far engaged in the necessary questioning of social structures and unequal gender relations. Instead it has continued to mobilise women as another support base for a ruling regime seeking its own consolidation and legitimacy.

Nzomo (1993) concludes Khasiani and Njiro's (1993) collection on the Kenyan women's movement in similar vein, describing the movement as 'muzzled and toothless'. She observes that despite their numerically high membership, the Women's Bureau (MYWO) and the National Council of Women of Kenya (NCWK) have been ineffective in empowering women and advancing their participation in decision-making. She attributes this to the fact that these organisations are controlled by conservative leaders who have consistently supported the ruling regime.

Likewise, Abdullah (1993) also decries the failure of women's organisations to address issues of gender subordination in Nigerian society, or to challenge the conservative agenda of government programmes like the Better Life Programme instituted under the Babangida regime. 'Military regimes' she writes 'are by their nature repressive and undemocratic and cannot therefore undertake responsibility for the liberation of any sector or group in society' (1993:32).

Mama (1995a), also writing on Nigeria, analyses the emergence, not of a women's movement, mass-based or otherwise, but of a femocracy. This she defines as a feminine autocracy paralleling and servicing a persistent military dictatorship, and advancing a highly conservative brand of gender politics in the name of 'women in development'. This argument reaches similarly pessimistic conclusions about the likelihood of existing organizational forms challenging women's oppression or advancing women's political, social or economic interests.

What then are the prospects for women's involvement in the state and politics in the coming years? This is clearly an area for more study. So far, only one collection of seminar papers (Kabira *et al.* 1993) is addressed to the future prospects, and this attempts to consider women's likely role in electoral party politics[2]. In it women scholars respond to the introduction of multipartyism in Kenya. They discuss the possibilities democratisation may afford women in the areas of health (Ngechu), reproductive rights (Khasiani), education (Mukudi; Obura), culture and language (Mukabi-Kabira; Odhiambo-Oduol; Ngechu), and political life (contributions by Nzomo; Kameri-Mbote et al. and Gachukia). However, there is no critical discussion of whether Kenyan multipartyism is likely to translate into fully-fledged democracy, something which seems to be assumed by the contributors. Nor are we informed about the actual involvement of women in party politics. Nzomo (1993:7) introduces the collection by defining a democratic political system as 'one which encourages and makes possible the free and voluntary involvement of the people in the political life of the nation', noting that only approximations of this ideal have ever been achieved. She argues that women must be involved as much as men for a system to be truly democratic. Citing facts and figures to prove that Kenyan women have been completely marginalised from politics and public decision-making, she goes on to list a series of strategies for overcoming this history. One of these strategies is the formation of a strong and autonomous women's movement, a development which would facilitate the political education and mobilization of women and the identification of women candidates.

Recent research carried out in predominantly Muslim areas of Africa has centred around comparison of the gender politics of the nationalist period and those of the contemporary period, during which the rise of Islamist movements has undermined the dominance of secular and socialist discourses. The struggle between secular nationalism and Islamism appear to be most pronounced in the Algerian case (see Lazreg 1990, Knauss 1992, Cheriet ·1992, Tlemcani 1992, Baffoun 1994, Bouatta & Cherifati-Merabtie 1994). It is however, also a key theme in gender-aware studies of the state and politics carried out in Tunisia (Baffoun 1994),

---

2   The Kabira *et al.* (1993) collection has a misleading title *Democratic Change in Africa: Women's Perspective* it contains only Kenyan material and is not Africa-wide in its conceptualisation.

Egypt (Badran 1994, Shukrullah 1994), Sudan (Hale 1993) and Senegal (Creevey 1991, Callaway and Creevey 1994).

The main themes of this literature can be illustrated with reference to the Algerian studies, which are by far the most detailed. Particularly outstanding is Lazreg's (1990, 1994) work, which furnishes us with a thorough case study of Algerian women's situation from pre-colonial times to the present. She re-analyses the gender politics of the nationalist discourse espoused by the FLN to highlight the ways in which they accommodated conventional notions of femininity. She distances herself from the Western feminist analysis which implies that Algerian women were duped into participating in a revolution which then betrayed them, providing a more balanced and nuanced understanding of the gender politics of Algerian nationalism.

During the war, in which over 10,000 women are on record as having worked for the FLN, most were in the civilian service where they performed tasks that were 'less spectacular, perhaps even tedious, but equally dangerous' (Lazreg 1994:124), taking charge of food, medical and weapons supplies and the underground network of sanctuaries, and washing clothes for the fighters. Only 11 per cent of the military wing were women, mostly serving as nurses. Very few engaged in highly publicized paramilitary acts of destruction or combat, and it is hard to make sense of the reluctance showed by the FLN on the question of arming nurses working in combat zones for their own protection. Casualties were high for both sexes: as many as one woman in five was either imprisoned or killed by the French during the war. The fact that more than half of the women registered with the Ministry of War Veterans who were killed were under twenty five years of age indicates that many of those who joined up were young, single women who did not have children they would have had to leave.

Lazreg (1994:140) concludes that priority had to be given to driving out the French, and in any case, women did not voice concerns that would be considered as 'feminist' today. Instead they tended to assume that 'they would naturally be recognised later'. These factors, combined with the complete absence of women in the leadership are used to explain why the FLN failed to take any concrete steps to redress gender inequality.

At the end of the war, victory was characterised by a restorationist rather than a revolutionary mood, with young vigilantes, and Mohammed Khider, the leader of the FLN, ushering women back to the kitchens. No women served on the FLN Central Committee, either during Ben Bella's government

(1962-1965) or during Boumediene's (1965-1978). Nor has any woman ever sat on the National Council of the Revolution. In 1968, the National Union of Algerian Women, formed in 1962, was incorporated and subordinated to the FLN (Knauss 1994, Lazreg 1994).

Lazreg's astute analysis of Algerian nationalism is followed by a well-researched consideration of how women have fared under the different regimes that have governed Algeria since independence. She tells us that, broadly speaking, after independence, official statements and documents suggest that while FLN government might have initially intended to pursue the gains made by women through their participation in the war, they never got beyond polemic. The 1964 Charter of Algiers, for example, made general recommendations, but the only concrete prescriptions for women pertained to widows' pensions. Lazreg (1994:146) sums up the early 1960s period thus: women, as a group, were seen as necessary to the building of the state, but as contributors, not participants. Sacrifice, not duty complemented by right, was the cornerstone of the new state's view of women.

Subsequently, neither the National Charter (1976) nor the successive constitutions have committed the state to defending women's rights.

More generally, early commitments to socialism have been superseded by a capitalist economy and a rhetorical liberalism more concerned with appeasing the growing Islamic brotherhoods than with challenging them. Until the 1980s, gender relations provided an uncontested site of compromise.

The Family Code was drafted in the 1970s, but not passed until 1984, largely because it proved so contentious, not only to women, but also to conservative and liberal men, for different reasons. For women it heralded the institutionalization of the gender inequality that had increasingly been encroaching on their lives over the previous two decades. Public demonstrations and lobbying made feminist activity visible for the first time. Women were unable to prevent the passage of the Code, and the fact that it took this codification of sharia law to draw women out of their political stupor is telling. However, this setback has also provoked the emergence of a small but independent women's movement which Lazreg regards with optimism.

What the afore-mentioned studies of gender politics in predominantly Muslim African states show is a pattern in which nationalist and secular forces have repeatedly given ground on gender issues in futile efforts to appease and accommodate the gathering forces of political Islamists. This they have done by condoning the reassertion of patriarchal values and institutionalizing gender inequality, often in the name of cultural authenticity.

South African studies on women and gender display the most radical gender politics in the region. Unapologetic in their commitment to women's liberation, and their discussion of feminism, South African scholarship displays great awareness of the failings of African national liberation struggles when it comes to the question of gender equality. Perhaps because there is a long tradition of activist scholarship in the region, women scholars here have not hesitated to be critical of the conservatism that has, at least until recently, characterised the gender politics of African as well as Afrikaner nationalism. Occasional progressive statements in favour of women's participation in the struggle notwithstanding, several authors have drawn attention to the unreconstructed practice of politics: the exclusion of women from leadership positions within the nationalist movement, and the official view that women's liberation is a divisive issue that must only be considered insofar as it facilitates, and remains subordinate to, national liberation (Hassim 1991, McClintock 1995, McFadden 1992). Until the end of the 1980s at least, it was pertinent to pose the question: 'Why has the oldest anti-colonial struggle on the African continent not moved beyond the conventional nationalist position on gender?' (McFadden 1992:512)

Several researchers have homed in on the way in which ideologies of motherhood have been mobilized, not just by conservative forces such as the Afrikaner nationalist organisations and the Inkatha Freedom Party, but also by the African National Congress (ANC) (e.g. Gaitskell and Unterhalter 1989, McClintock 1995). In focusing on one of women's roles to the exclusion of others, all such ideologies fix women in accordance with their biological proclivities, and ignore the fact that, important though motherhood may be to many women, not all women are mothers, and many women are other things besides the producers of subsequent generations of Zulu, Boers or African nationalists.

South African studies of gender and national politics have examined the momentous changes of the last few years from a gender perspective. Whereas some retain a healthy cynicism with respect to the prospects for women in a new and democratic South Africa, at least one analyst finds grounds for optimism. Seidman (1993) draws our attention to the structure of the South African economy, in which over one third of African women are employed in the formal economy (1985 figures), making South African women the most proletarianised in the region. She also extols the high level of independent political organisation by women at local and community levels, and the extent to which feminist activists within the nationalist movement have managed to push the debate on gender forward and into the public eye over the last few years, despite the historical conservatism of the ANC Women's League. In analysing the changes within the Confederation of South African Trade Unions (COSATU) and the ANC, she concludes that since the beginning of the 1990's there has been a qualitative change in gender politics, emanating not so much from the political leaders as from community organisations and rank and file women. Issues formerly ignored by the mainstream — domestic relations, sexual harassment and women's representation in decision-making — are no longer deferred quite as easily as they have been in the past. In 1991 for example, the ANC Women's League, long viewed as a 'ladies auxiliary organisation' chose to insist on a 30 per cent quota of women to be elected to the national executive committee of the ANC. The fact that rank and file men, comprising 83 per cent the membership successfully opposed the motion until it was withdrawn does not detract from the fact that the issue was raised, and provoked the most heated debate at the entire conference. Her evidence suggests that in the South African case at least:

> [...]feminist demands within the South African nationalist movement emanate not from a few educated women or the national leadership but from within precisely the popular base from which the ANC draws its support' (Seidman 1993: 315).

McClintock (1995) builds on these earlier analyses, beginning her discussion of gender and race in South African politics by reconsidering theories of nationalism. Taking up Benedict Anderson's oft-cited theorisation of nations as 'imagined communities', she draws our attention to the way in which the imagination behind nations have invariably been masculine. She prefaces her critique of nationalism with Enloe's remark that nationalisms have 'typically sprung from masculinized memory, masculine humiliation and masculinized hope' (Enloe 1989:44), and reminds us that while male theorists of nationalism might have been blind to gender (with the notable exception of Frantz Fanon), feminists, for their part, have only recently begun to seriously engage with issues of ethnicity and nationality (as has been pointed out by Yuval Davis and Anthias 1989, Enloe 1989, and other feminist theorists). With particular reference to his essay 'Algeria Unveiled', she correctly points out that Fanon's analysis, while not gender blind, is far from feminist, and remains unable to theorise female agency as anything other than appended to that of men, and is therefore unable to construe women as historical actors in their own right.

McClintock (1995:357) proceeds to lay out four things that a feminist theory of nationalism might take on: i) investigating the gendered formation of sanctioned male theories; ii) bringing into historical visibility women's active cultural and political participation in national formations; iii) bringing nationalist institutions into critical relation with other social structures and institutions; and iv) paying scrupulous attention to the structures of racial, ethnic and class power that continue to bedevil privileged forms of feminism. The remainder of her discussion reconsiders Afrikaner nationalism as an invention that is as profoundly patriarchal as it is racist, offering more detail than the preceding analyses (Gaitskell and Unterhalter 1989, Seidman 1993, MacFadden 1992, Hassim 1991). Little wonder then that the Boers fashioned a system that African women have struggled so long and hard against, mobilizing whatever identities and cultural resources they have been able to invoke, as Africans and as women. Finally she discusses recent developments in the relationship between feminism and nationalism in South Africa, drawing attention to the fact that black women, once shy of being labelled divisive, are now more confidently demanding the right to fashion a nationalist feminism in terms of their own needs and situations, within and beyond the ANC.

More generally, scholarship on women, gender and the African state over the last five years shows a growing attention to the dynamic interaction between state and society, and between competing groups within civil society. Even though the concept of the state is still monolithically patriarchal, society begins to be viewed as comprising men and women, with women's actions and responses having unforeseen effects on the male-dominated state, and the relationship between women and the state combining various degrees of autonomy and reciprocity. This change in emphasis is partly an effect of the different disciplinary and methodological influences that studies of women and the state display. Not being limited to macrosociological methods, women's studies have introduced micro sociological techniques, and these have in turn brought new insights. Even the most oppressed and marginalised groups are seen as actors rather than passive recipients of whatever the state metes out to the people. Key features and dimensions of state-society relations, the relationships between what is official and what is unofficial, what is formal and informal, and between the centre and the periphery - are all illuminated through the lens of gender.

The state itself must then be viewed as a site of contestation, an entity embedded in complex relationships of reciprocity and conflict with different social groups. The 'woman question' has generally been treated opportunistically and exploitatively by insecure regimes on the one hand wishing to retain credibility within the international community, but on the other, seeking to authenticate themselves with populist appeals to anachronistic notions of masculinity. With this more nuanced understanding of state processes comes an extension of the boundaries of what is deemed to be political, which in turn demands an expansion of the African political science agenda. No longer can political science be limited to the study of the formal and public sphere, but instead it must also address the dialectics of private and public life, of the household and the community, of the formal and the informal.

There are also great gaps in the literature. While a great many seminars have been held on women and politics, or women and democracy, these have tended to focus on multipartyism and mobilizing women to run and vote in elections. Meanwhile, a subject as pertinent as gender and militarism remains neglected. Nor are there many studies on the participation of women in the purported clan and ethnic disturbances. What role have women played in the destruction of states, and what will a gender analyses of the genocidal regimes in central Africa uncover? Media footage suggests that Liberian politics is an all-male affair, but is this indeed the case, and if it is, where are the women of Liberia and what are they doing?

The above mentioned studies of gender politics in contemporary African states all agree that women's interests would best be advanced by the existence of national, independent and united women's movements. Several draw attention to instances where this has been an effective check on the unmitigated assertion or re-assertion of patriarchy. The analyses put forward however are more informative on what has gone before and what should be avoided than on current situations and how women's involvement might be strengthened. Politically, African women are no longer novices, but it seems they still have much to overcome.

Cultural Studies

A significant proportion of the research on African women carried out in the 1990s looks at the various aspects of women's lives, and their role in the production and reproduction of culture, and thus falls under the cross-disciplinary rubric of cultural studies. The interest in matters of culture may be partly due to the fact that many more women social scientists have backgrounds in anthropology, history, psychology or sociology than in the drier disciplines of economics, political science or international relations. It can also be traced to the methodological innovations of women's studies which have favoured the use of ethnographic methods, biographies and oral histories, all methods more amenable to the holistic and cross-disciplinary analyses characteristic of cultural studies. A third possible cause of the popularity of cultural studies lies in the fact that 'culture' has long been identified as that pervasive terrain on which patriarchy manifests, resisting change and perpetuating women's oppression. Changing the long-standing cultural practices the traditions and customs which sustain and reproduce gender inequality is therefore fundamental to the agenda of women's movements worldwide, and research is often viewed as a necessary prelude to such change. The reverse is also true: it is where attempts are made to change cultural practice that the status quo most clearly springs into view and tradition asserts itself most strongly. This means that feminist activism itself has often led to the revelation and reassertion of patriarchal culture, reinforcing the choice of culture as a worthy target of feminist scholarship.

Although ethnographic work has often been sensitive to gender, early studies were often imbued with patriarchal biases resulting from the male dominance of the discipline, the reliance on male informants and the preconceptions that researchers from patriarchal Western societies carried over into their analysis. The earliest studies of African women however, (e.g. Paulme 1963) introduced a focus on women's power in traditional societies which is evident in many of the more recent studies. Cultural studies of African women have begun to address the dynamism, diversity and complexity of gender relations undergoing rapid change, as well as producing detailed analyses of the changes wrought in women's lives and realities by a range of political, economic and social forces.

One of the recurring themes of literature on women and culture is that of domesticity.

Ideologies of Domesticity

While 'domestic' literally means of the home or family, or a household servant, when applied to Africans the less obvious meaning 'to bring under human control, tame or civilise' introduces a nuance that captures much about the various colonial efforts to instil in African women anachronistic values regarding work and social graces.

Hansen's (1992) *African Encounters with Domesticity* is a collection which addresses colonial attempts to 'domesticate' African women, efforts directed towards the creation of a select cadre of 'suitable wives' for that class of African men entering in colonial service as clerks and junior administrators. Walker's (1990) collection includes several chapters addressing the role of mission settlements and elite schools in furthering this end in South Africa. Hunt (1990) is a study of the social clubs that were set up to domesticate 'native' women in the then Belgian Congo. These organisations were not explicitly designed government agencies: they emerged instead out of the 'good intentions' of the wives of missionaries and colonial officials, intentions which happened to resonate with the wider designs of the imperialists (see also Musisi 1992 on Uganda, Denzer 1992 on Yorubaland, Ranchard-Nilsson 1992 on Southern Rhodesia). The colonial state welcomed a development which was to see at least a section of African womanhood being trained in the social graces of Victorian fashion and etiquette, cake making, needlecraft and flower arranging. The ideology of domesticity was also a way of ensuring that women's reproductive work remained outside the public sphere, so enabling the appropriation of labour that had been so integral to the development of Western capitalism. That this sometimes resonated with indigenous African traditions of female domesticity is amply demonstrated in the literature on African households [see for example Mack's (1992) discussion of harem domesticity in Kano, Nigeria]. The literature on ideologies of domesticity generally suggests that while African women traditionally had clearly defined tasks and responsibilities that were no less important, even though distinct from, those of men, European influences narrowed these down to housewifery, and tolerated only a limited amount of charity work in the community. Women were not expected to be, or accepted as, the highly productive farmers, traders and manufacturers that many of them were. The inculcation of the ideology of domesticity accompanied the development of a cash economy. Acting in consonance, these two changes had profound effects on women: their productive work and their contributions to both the wider economy and the sustenance of their households became less and less visible, and increasingly uncounted and unremunerated (see the later discussion of women's work).

Most of the research on the gender ideology of domesticity is concerned with the role of the colonial state and missions in the housewifisation of elite African women (*see* discussion of Christianity below). Less attention has been given to the ideologies of domesticity conveyed through indigenous cultures, through Islam and through other religions (animism, indigenous Christianity, ancient coptic churches, Hinduism in East and Southern Africa, Judaism and orthodox Christianity in North East Africa). These too unhesitatingly ascribe limited and specific purposes to women, most of which are rooted in essentialist, often biological, beliefs about femininity and female sexuality.

Women, Religion, Resistance

Religion has been a popular subject of study, presumably because religion, like custom, is a major vehicle for gender ideologies that oppress women. Feminists are in agreement that, on the balance, all the major religious texts have provided justifications for the oppression of women and assertions of male superiority, whether one regards these as intrinsic to the texts themselves, or as the logical result of men's success in appropriating these texts.

A number of studies address women's situation in Islamic cultures. The research on Christianity does not generally treat the faith as a 'culture' *per se*, but rather is comprised of smaller, more intimate studies of the activities of particular missions, or churches. This may be because most of the major studies published in English have been carried out by Western scholars who are more distant from Islam. Furthermore, until recently, the most detailed studies of women and Islam have been carried out on middle-Eastern rather than African societies, the best known exceptions being the work of the Egyptian writer, Nawal El Sadaawi and Fatima Mernissi in Morocco.

There are very few recent studies of the role of women in African traditional belief systems and religions (but see e.g. Amadiume 1987), and major texts on African philosophy make little reference to gender (e.g. Hountoundji 1983). However, it has often been asserted that traditional African societies were matriarchal, and a contrast drawn between 'primitive' matriarchies and 'civilised' patriarchies. African scholars have also argued that women were more powerful in indigenous religions than in the more recently arrived monotheistic faiths (e.g. Diop 1974: 142-145, Amadiume 1987).

Post-feminist interest in studying the effects of Islam on women may also be motivated by concern to test the widely held assumption that Islam has generally been more oppressive to women than other religions, a position that has gained currency with the contemporary proliferation of islamist movements which re-assert conservative gender ideologies. This assumption is questioned from time to time, but not really laid to rest by the evidence presented in Callaway and Creevey (1994) in *The Heritage of Islam*.

Addressing itself to 'women, religion and politics in West Africa', this study relies primarily on data gathered in Senegal and Nigeria with only occasional reference to other countries in the sub-region. The comparative framework they use compares the various forms of Islam practised in Senegal (Wolof, Serer, Tukulor and Dyola), not with the various forms of Islam practised in Nigeria, but with the Islamic culture of the Kano Hausa in northern Nigeria. This creates the impression that Senegalese Islam is relatively favourable to women, a position which would not had been upheld had they either limited themselves to an inter-ethnic comparison of say, Tukulor Islam with Hausa Islam, or compared the various forms of Islam that exist in the two countries. In defence of Nigerian Islam, one would not challenge their observation that the Hausa Muslim interpretation is amongst the most conservative in Africa, but rather draw attention to the fact that most Nigerian Muslims are not Kano Hausa. Islam is practiced differently by the very large Yoruba and Nupe communities and numerous other ethnic groups, not to mention the Hausa communities residing elsewhere in Nigeria[3]

In Senegal, where Islam has been established for longer than amongst the Hausa Muslims of Northern Nigeria, it has also been tempered by the French insistence on limiting the influence of Islam on the national body politic. Another distinctive feature of Senegalese Islam that Callaway and Creevey draw attention to is the system of brotherhoods, some of which allow women to play a greater practical role in public affairs than the Kano Muslims. Although they are not technically accepted as members of

---

[3] Even within Kano state the practice of Islam varies, with the ruling Hausa-Fulani elite observing restrictions on women's participation in public life, and practicing the seclusion of women far more stringently than the talakawa (Hausa peasantry).

brotherhoods, women do identify themselves as belonging to them. They also consult marabouts about their problems as often as men if not more, and play active roles in the social and religious life of their communities.

Much of what Callaway and Creevey have to say centres around the question of whether religion shapes or reflects society. They find partial answers in their discussion of traditional cultures, women's education, their roles in the formal and informal economies and questions of political empowerment, all of which shape women's lives and preclude arrogating to Islam the power to determine. This analysis takes us some way beyond the simplistic notion that Islam is the source of women's oppression in the Muslim world. Instead they have generated an interactive account in which the influence of Islam continuously combines with old and new cultural forces which can, but by implication need not necessarily, subordinate women. Nonetheless, it is clear that women are far from equal to men even in the 'more progressive' Islamic context of modern Senegal. Where women have made the greatest advances, it is not due to Islam, but to the mitigation of the effects of Islam by indigenous and foreign influences. Nonetheless, the fact that it is primarily a comparative study of Islam still generates the impression that differences between Senegal and Nigeria are based in religion. This point can be illustrated by contrasting the relatively unrestrained politics of the Senegalese Muslim feminist organisation Yeewi-Yeewi with the careful conduct and conservative tone taken by Nigeria's Federation of Muslim Women (FOMWAN). The difference between the two is more likely to be a result of the contrasting national political cultures than to locally-specific manifestations of Islam. Yeewi-Yeewi exists in a long-standing multiparty state with a high level of public political debate, whereas FOMWAN has thrived alongside a military dictatorship, in a nation characterised by religious nepotism.

Generally speaking, the recent studies published on Islam in West Africa (Creevey 1991, Callaway and Creevey 1994, and Imam 1994) afford us a more nuanced understanding of the impact of Islam on the lives of specific groups of African women - one which acknowledges that Islam has both undermined and strengthened women's position in society at different historical moments, but has always had its effect in conjunction with other variables. In other words, religion does not operate as a determining factor on its own, and it is therefore virtually impossible to assert whether a given faith, or a particular interpretation of a faith, is more or less favourable to women as compared to another.

Other studies have focused on the corrosive effects of Islamic fundamentalism on women's situation in various African countries, including the Sudan (Hale 1992), Egypt (Badran 1994, Shukrallah 1994), Algeria (Lazreg), Bouatta and Cherifati-Merabtie 1994) and Tunisia (Baffoun 1994)[4] Gender has clearly been a key site for the production and proliferation of Islamic fundamentalist ideologies. The circumscription and curtailment of women's activities and visibility has characterised militant Islam in all the countries under study.

Shukrallah (1994) outlines the conditions giving rise to the emergence of the Egyptian Islamic movement, arguing that the failure of modernization for the majority of the people has led to a crisis in nationalist secular discourse. More than this however, she draws attention to the way in which the leadership of the nationalist movement compromised on the gender question, never really upholding the right of women to be full citizens in the emerging nation-state. It seems that ever since that time, Egyptian women have faced contradictions between their status as citizens of a supposedly secular nation-state, and their explicitly circumscribed status within the *umma*. Within conservative Islamic discourse they are cast as bearers of authenticity, and subjected to a narrow, reified identity.

Also writing on Egypt, Badran (1994) looks at the different discourses positioning feminists, pro-feminists (women with feminist sympathies who do not wish to be publicly known as such) and Islamist women. She uses the term 'gender activism' to accommodate the fact that there are competing discourses on femininity emanating from these different groupings. Badran (1994) notes that the rise of conservatism in Egypt occurred during the 1970s, just as the feminism was resurging internationally, a coincidence which has augmented the polarisation of Islam and feminism in Egypt. In today's conservative-dominated Egypt, feminists speak with a muted voice and are reluctant to declare themselves to be proponents of women's liberation, whereas Islamists (women and men alike) are stridently proclaiming their avowedly anti-feminist prescriptions for a quintessential 'Muslim woman'. Islamist discourse on women disowns the proud history of Egyptian women, casting early pioneers like Huda Sharaawi as morally corrupt, and insisting that women's rights are better protected within Islam, and from behind the veil. The main

---

4   these studies are also discussed in the section on State and Politics.

role of these gender activists is the mobilization of women for the Islamic movement, but it is their efforts to secure women's rights, as prescribed by Islam which qualifies them for Badran's (1994) use of the term gender activists. It is an era which differs markedly from the 1920s, when Egyptian feminists held the centre of the public stage [4] within and beyond the boundaries of the nation.

Badran (1994) identifies a third, younger and more intellectual group whom she dubs 'Islamist feminists', comprising women who are reluctant to reject feminist thought entirely. Instead they adopt a strategy of critical engagement, cross-referring to the Qu'ran in an effort to isolate and appropriate acceptable elements of feminist thought. Less scornful of other women's struggles, they call for a movement to liberate women from within Islam, and engage in the ideological task of reinterpreting the Qu'ran and the hadiths.[5]

Boutta and Cherifati-Merabtine (1994) analyze the Front Islamique du Salut (FIS) newspaper *El Mounquid* as a way of investigating the representation of women in Algeria's Islamist movement. Although this organ officially denies the need for any consideration of 'the woman question' on the basis that 'Islam has provided all rights to the woman' its pages are nonetheless replete with articles prescribing Muslim femininity. The new 'Muslim woman' is construed in manner which is both detailed and contradictory. She is simultaneously celebrated as being superior to all other women, and subjected to a series of taboos, all of which are viewed as leading to depravity and a return to the ever-threatening Jahilia (pre-Islamic state of ignorance). Like the Egyptian and other Islamists, the writers of *El Mounquid* use biological arguments to justify these taboos: women are the psychological and physical inferiors of men, born to be wives and mothers, and who should be kept hidden under the heavy cloth of honour and purity the hijab. Like the Egyptian and Tunisian scholars cited above, these authors point out that this simplistic and static construction of Islamic femininity denies both the diverse realities that constitute modern women's lives and the collective history in which the *moudjahidates* played a heroic role in the war for national liberation.[6]

---

5   A similar exercise is carried out under the auspices of the international network Women Living Under Muslim Law.
6   The discussion of Marnia Lazreg's book on Algerian women in the section on State and politics.

Hale's penetrating analysis of the Sudanese Islamic movement explores the role of women in the National Islamic Front (NIF). According to this, the elite women who have become the Front's main spokeswomen derive certain benefits from their activities. She argues that the presence of a few high profile women in the movement is not so much an emancipatory development, as a reflection of the class interests that underpin the apparently devout concerns of the NIF. Amongst other things, the NIF is engaged in the very worldly business of negotiating a new sexual division of labour which selectively removes women from prestigious professional positions, while allowing less privileged women to continue to work in unrewarding menial capacities, when and as needed, to support their families. It is a contradictory renegotiation which accommodates the realities of an economic crisis that has resulted in fewer men than ever being able to live up to the ideal of keeping their wives at home. Ultimately this re-negotiation ensures that women can still be exploited in marginalised sectors of the labour market while denying them any significant place in public life.

Accommodating Protest (Macleod 1991) is a rich and detailed study of the lives of lower middle class working women in Cairo. She examines the material and ideological conditions which have given rise to the phenomenon that has been dubbed the 'new veiling'. In the best methodological tradition of women's studies, Macleod spent years living and socialising with the women she writes about with such sensitivity. She presents her findings in a clearly-written and unpretentious manner which allows an intimate level of identification between reader and researched. Although like Hale, Macleod has an eye for the contradictions between Islamist discourse and socio-economic realities, the women in her study are very clearly not just victims of macrosociological forces, but architects of their own destinies. The openness of her methodology allows us to comprehend the deliberate manner in which those who are adopting the new veiling weigh up their situation and make a choice. Here are women who will don the veil in an attempt to resolve the contradictions they experience between working outside the home and remaining respectable, in a socially conservative climate. Perhaps this is why the veils they wear are modified: no longer a uniform black cover, the modern veil has become the bedrock of a flourishing indigenous fashion industry. A range of elegant stylistic variations allow a much fuller expression of individuality, one that is not a mere mimicry of either Western fashion or the Middle Eastern hijab.

It is the series of compromises and innovations that the new veiling encompasses that has led Macleod to develop the idea of 'accommodating protest'. On the one hand, veiling appears to reinstate old values regarding women's role and identity. On the other, veiling can be viewed as a form of protest, one of a number of 'unusual forms of struggle' available to groups for whom strikes and public demonstrations would be inappropriate. The new veiling is a style of struggle that is 'an ambivalent mixture of acquiescence, protest and accommodation', one which 'perfectly conveys women's contradictory intentions' (Macleod 1991:127). Lower middle class working women, compelled to work for money, lose out in the absence of a modern identity which would impute value to their lives. So they wear the veil worn by more affluent middle class women in an effort to recover some of the dignity and respect afforded to housewives in traditional society. It is therefore at best an ambiguous form of protest which risks perpetuating the inequality that women experience, but one which illustrates the nebulous character of women's oppression, and women's recognition of the fact that their menfolks too are enmeshed in a web of power relations. An over-simple Gramscian reading of this action would suggest that working women are supporting a dominant ideology and consenting to patriarchal hegemony. It is Macleod's attention to the ambivalence and contradictions experienced by lower middle class working women, that precludes such an interpretation, favouring the more nuanced reading that she makes.

It is a fascinating study which reveals some of the constant negotiations and changes that are occurring in urban Egypt at the present time as a result of unique conjunctions of international and local forces.

Much remains to be investigated regarding the legacies of centuries of Judaeo-Christian influences in Africa. Christianity has presented itself as uplifting and progressive, emphasizing the role of mission schools in educating and raising the 'heathen'. In opposition to this view, anti-imperialists and cultural nationalists alike have argued that the European religion played a key role in the subjugation of African people, derogating indigenous cultures and instilling a psychology of self-hatred and contempt for African ways. Gender analysis of the legacies of Christianity throws new light on the whole debate, revealing a complex and varied picture in which there were both gains and losses in women's status, changes which were part and parcel of changes in notions of masculinity and femininity, the sexual division of labour and in marital and sexual practices. All of these were inextricably intertwined with the radical transformations that accompanied the different stages and forms that colonialism took at different moments and in different places. Not only did the impact of Christianity depend on what existing gender relations were like, but also on the class and caste position of the women in question. Exemplary historical studies have been carried out in South Africa, using official records and archival sources to investigate aspects of missionary communities, schools and church organisations between the 1800s and 1945 (Meintjes 1990, Hughes 1990 and Gaitskell 1990).

Meintjes (1990) examines the changes in gender relations in a 19th century Wesleyan settlement in Natal, noting that the doctrine introduced by James Allison, catechist and missionary, was not passively imbibed by the multi-ethnic community that constituted Edendale. Here the contact between Wesleyan Christianity and traditional norms yielded a synthesis that was largely governed by the exigencies of survival in a changing colonial economy. While the Wesleyans favoured the exclusion of women from work outside the home, African women were traditionally engaged in agricultural labour, with the result that African women ended up performing an arduous combination of domestic tasks decreed by Christianity and poorly remunerated farm labour decreed by tradition. Boys were taught wagon-making and masonry, girls tutored in the skills required of 'angels of the house', namely cooking, food preserving, making Victorian clothes and laundering. African women, far from being lifted out of drudgery, were encouraged to be subservient, and found themselves dutifully combining these additional domestic chores with animal rearing, hoeing, weeding, harvesting, food storage, the making of mattresses and so forth.

Although Christian marriage rites were introduced, African marriages continued to be governed under repressive customary laws which afforded women the status of minors, to be kept under the full control of their fathers, then their husbands, and on widowhood, their husbands brothers or even their own sons. Those women who undertook paid work (often before, between or after marriages) invariably found themselves falling back on domestic skills: taking in laundry, becoming maids or seamstresses. As if seeking a positive note in this scenario of female servitude, Meintjes ends with a mention of the new possibilities for socialising that church groups created. These women are said to have taken great pride in their cooking and sewing and to have found avenues for self expression in their homes and elaborate dress styles.

Hughes' (1990) is a study of the establishment of the first boarding school for African girls. As a school for the daughters of the African elite, the Inanda seminary (1869-1945) developed a unique emphasis on academic education, at a time when most girls' schools restricted education to training suitable for future maids. Nonetheless the perceived options, even for relatively privileged African women, centred around the dominant notion of femininity: they were to be helpmates to their husbands, teachers or nurses. Hughes (1990) presents a fascinating study of the obsessive concern to regulate the femininity and control the sexuality of the favoured daughters of converts. The conflicts that these girls experienced and the insights they had into their world are glimpsed through her original use of excerpts taken from school essays.

The highly visible and active participation of women in African church organisations at times appears to suggest that there are instances of Christianity empowering African women, an argument taken up by Gaitskell when she concludes her study of *manyanos*, the highly popular and cohesive women's unions that accompanied the spread of Christianity to urban areas. Engaging in evangelical and fund-raising activities, and adopting an enthusiastic revivalist style of praying and preaching, these organisations appear to have been partly responsible for the preponderance of women converts. She discusses the different motivations that men and women had for converting, suggesting that whereas men may have more often been seeking self-improvement, women may have more often been 'refugees' from tradition, fleeing to mission compounds to avoid forced marriages, escape domestic violence or avoid the misery of widowhood. However, having converted, women at best received a 'contradictory package', with their traditional powerlessness being replaced by subjection to Christian patriarchy and domesticity. It is in this context that Church unions seem to have offered women both a means of self-expression and release and a potential means of empowerment, while at the same time introducing clearly African variants of Christianity.

Studies of the Christianity in contemporary Africa have continued to show the various churches having contradictory results for African women, sometimes facilitating their oppression and sometimes offering a means of protection or even, on occasion, empowerment, whether through granting women access to Western education, or through women's direct participation in church activities and networks. While historical research focuses on missions, contemporary studies draw attention to the complex interplay of gender and power within the newer African churches.

Crumbley (1992) for example, looks at the role of women in the indigenous Christian movement that has given rise to the Aladura churches in Nigeria. Characterised by the central role of prophet healers, belief in divine revelation, faith healing and the efficacy of prayer to change material circumstances, and incorporating features of Yoruba traditional religion, the Aladura churches have proliferated in and beyond West Africa. Crumbley looks at three denominations: the Celestial Church of Christ, The Christ Apostolic Church and the Church of the Lord-Aladura. Only the Church of the Lord-Aladura allows women to play leadership roles, having parallel male and female offices at each level of its structure, and training both prophets and prophetesses. Regarding itself as a progressive and pace-setting church, it is radically different from the Christ Apostolic Church and the Celestial Church of Christ, both of which observe such strict menstrual taboos that women are excluded from religious participation for a significant proportion of the month. Even when they are allowed to participate, women are forbidden to speak unless called upon. In discussing the different 'ideologies of impurity' in these different churches, Crumbley just illustrates now complex cultural analysis must be if it is to take historical and structural ambiguities as well as cultural legacies into account.

Marshall (1991) analyses the rise to religious and social prominence of the newer charismatic or Pentecostalist Christian movement, thousands of new churches and groups having been set up all over Southern Nigeria. Her analysis links the personal and social processes of rebirth to the creation of autonomous spaces which defy existing power monopolies and propagate new power relations, thus presenting new opportunities for survival. Despite the doctrinal emphasis on women's domestic obligations, being a born-again woman does offer some avenues for empowerment. Women adherents find themselves equipped to resist the demands for sexual favours, even from the most powerful men, and furnished with grounds for demanding sexual restraint, marital fidelity and monogamy from their men-folk. In the context of the post-oil boom commoditisation of sexuality and the profligacy of urban men, the degree of control that these mores grant to women is exceptional. In addition to altering sexual politics, the movement also offers a way of replacing the disintegrating extended family system and old patron-client networks with relatively egalitarian and dignified systems of spiritual solidarity and mutual support. Marshall's study shows how the born-again community confers upon its members a spiritual power believed to be capable of transforming the social and material world as well as the individual, in otherwise confusing times.

Sexuality

Considering that sexuality has been a major area of interest within women's studies internationally, the first question one asks in surveying African women's studies is why there are so few studies of sexuality? Is it because the historical legacy of racist fascination with African's allegedly profligate sexuality has deterred researchers? Modern African societies, while displaying great diversity of sexual politics, seem to me to be more often repressed than liberated: homophobia is rampant, lesbianism hardly enters public discussion; child abuse, though widespread, is more often denied than acknowledged; and there are many contexts in which even mature, adult women feel obliged to conduct their relationships in a clandestine manner. For a woman, married or otherwise, to admit her sexual appetite is regarded as unseemly. In stark contrast to this, the sexual behaviour of elite men is seldom monogamous and largely extramarital, involving a great many liaisons based on wealth and power rather than on emotional or intellectual exchange. Nonetheless, sexual aberrations and transgressions are still treated with severity in many African communities, and the majority of ordinary African men are obliged to exercise a degree of restraint, whether for religious, economic or customary reasons. This suggests that colonial portrayals of Africans as profligate and hyper sexual reveal more about the minds of the colonials than their subjects. Nowadays, fascination with the sexuality of black people conveys just as much about the racial politics of imperialistic societies, in which other people are still subjugated, and racial boundaries remain erotogenic.

In short, sexuality research remains a minefield very few African scholars venture into. The historical record demonstrates that there are very good reasons for this.

Imperial Sexuality

McClintock's (1995) book *Imperial Leather* addresses the complex terrain of race, gender and sexuality during the colonial conquest. These interwoven themes have featured in cultural studies of the colonial era, ever since feminists began to analyze the prevalence of the metaphors of conquest, in which women stand for the lands and peoples to be subjugated, ravaged and despoiled. While Fanon may have psychoanalyzed this metaphor, it is feminist scholars who have pointed out that it elides the existence of women altogether: the colonisers enjoy an exclusive, racialised masculinity that is accentuated by their forages into far away exotic and erotic places, and the colonised men are simultaneously feminised and degraded. Feminist scrutiny has insisted on examining the gender politics of colonialism and nationalism, and on giving women a place in these stories.

What makes McClintock's study so powerful is the manner in which she combines psychoanalytic and historical methodologies in an analysis that uses pictorial, biographical and literary material to explore, and subvert, the complex machinations of imperial sexuality, both in the imperial heartland and in the colonies. Starting with the popular fiction of Rider Haggard, replete as it is with masculinist images of cruel breasts, dangerous female genitalia and penial forays into virgin lands, she puts forward an incisive analysis of relationships between white men and their maids, racial and sexual transvestism, and of the cult of domesticity and female fetishism in the imperial metropolis. Africa became the theatre in which the corollaries of these peculiar sexual mores were enacted and re-enacted, becoming commoditised through the burgeoning capitalist advertising industry. Patriarchy was indeed reinvented in the colonies, in bizarre and unhealthy ways.

Her final section, aptly entitled 'Dismantling the Master's House' is a fitting tribute to Audre Lorde, the African American lesbian writer, and a pioneering discussion of cultural resistance. Here she unravels the part played by the black consciousness movement, the Soweto Poets, and community theatres in the emergence of South Africa from decades of apartheid, in many ways a distillation of imperial culture, and its concomitant sexual perversions (see section on State and Politics for discussion of McClintock's work on nationalism and feminism).

Summers (1991) essay 'Intimate Colonialism' also addresses sexuality during the colonial period, analysing the politics of British interventions into the sexual and reproductive lives of the Buganda in Uganda between 1907 and 1925. The Buganda were valued twofold: as agents of indirect rule, and as a major source of labour in the colony. Like McClintock's work on imperial sexual politics, Summer's essay tells us much about the perverse preoccupations of the Europeans. Like Vaughan (1991), Summers examines colonial interventions that appeared to be medical, but beneath this foil, were more about instilling imperial notions of hygiene and motherhood than about curing the targeted diseases. Grossly exaggerated figures on the incidence of syphilis created a climate of panic, during which all manner of inhumane interventions could be and were justified. She cites the head of an investigating commission as claiming that the epidemic of syphilis was so severe 'that the entire population stands a good chance of being exterminated in a very few years, or left a degenerate race fit for nothing' (F.J. Lambkin, cited in Summers 1991:790). Painful intramuscular injections of mercury were advocated as treatment for a disease that was perceived as being associated with the alleged promiscuity and immorality of the Buganda, particularly the women. Missionaries were less 'medical' in their condemnation of the Buganda, some even observing that the epidemic had been created by the Europeans, but all agreeing that Christianity was the only means of saving the nation.

By the end of the World War I, coercive medical interventions and STD programmes had been largely superseded by a moral crusade, in the form of the 'Social Purity Campaign' which aimed to inculcate ideas of domesticity and family life. Motherhood programmes and girl's education were directed at reshaping families, a pernicious feat of social engineering which rode on the degradation of African women as less than fully human, and unfit to mother the children they bore. The Maternity Training School became the main institution executing the mission to civilise African family life. As a mission-run maternity system, it trained African women at centres throughout the country, indoctrinating them to combine antenatal care and midwifery with sermonizing. Summers lucidly unravels the contradictions and ambiguities that beset the programme, turning as it did on an imported notion of women as the spiritual, moral and reproductive centres of families, and taking these into the sphere of public policy and state intervention.

The Nation and the Family

The family has been a common trope through which the nation is conceptualised, as is signified by the numerous references to the 'motherland' of many revolutionary movements, or the 'fatherland' of the more militaristic nationalism displayed by Afrikanerdom and its Nazi antecedents. Religious movements too often invoke notions of family amongst adherents of a particular faith, as in the muslim *umma*, and the idea of brothers and sisters in Christ amongst Christians. Various manifestations of African nationalism too have utilized the metaphor of the family in their rhetoric, in highly gendered ways. Most of these have perpetuated notions of women that are contingent on their reproductive role, as mothers of the nation or mothers of the revolution (see Gaitskell and Unterhalter (1989), Staunton 1991, Cock 1992). We have seen that feminist theory has demanded that theorists of nationalism address the gendered nature of nations and nationalist ideologies. This rethinking has most often been undertaken under the rubric of sexuality.

Nationalisms and Sexualities (Parker et al. 1992) contains two contributions on Africa. The first (Cobham 1992) is a discussion of fictional representations of African nationalism, and documents the way in which male authors have either reinforced or challenged simplistic notions of the nation and national identity, notions which are always gendered, or as Cobham puts it 'misgendered'. Taking Nuruddin Farah's *Maps* as the text which subverts the legacies of earlier writings, she focuses on the way in which Farah destabilizes national and sexual boundaries, in a way which forces:

> a remapping of the terrain that would take more fully into account the complexity of the modern nation-state in Africa... [and]... challenge a Western paradigm of linearity and consolidation...by confronting and accepting the way in which any act or identity within human culture situates itself in relation to the fluctuating social forces that constitute its specific historical moment (1992:57).

The second contribution on Africa in the same volume addresses the controversial subject of AIDS, or 'African Aids', to be exact (Patton 1992). Patton exposes once again, the Western ideological preoccupation with foisting the bourgeois, patriarchal family structure on Africa, this time as the 'preferred prophylaxis' against the modern scourge of AIDS. Patton argues that 'African AIDS' has been invented to distinguish this supposedly heterosexual disease from AIDS in the Western metropolis, in such a way that Western heterosexual masculinity is absolved of any need to change. Heterosexual AIDS is the AIDS of Others, who are alleged to have contracted the virus through bestiality and propagated it through promiscuity. Relying on a representation of Africa as a homogenous block, AIDS research has been directed by assumptions about Africans that are apparently innocuous or simply fantastic. AIDS manuals for use in Africa betray a stereotyped and unsubstantiated portrayal of African sexuality as different from Western sexuality: homosexuality hardly exists, but heterosexual promiscuity is everywhere, and African men will not use condoms. An idealised 'rural family' is nostalgically invoked, in portrayals which obscurse a reality in which polygamy and non-marital sexual practices exist in numerous forms.

The above contributions to our understanding of sexuality in contemporary Africa reveal it to be a site of contested representations, in which few facts are available to rebuff contradictory and derogatory assumptions about Africans, a place dogged by imperialist\attempts to engineer the reorganization of diverse cultures and social relations into sanitized and controllable nuclear families. Ideologies of domesticity have been accompanied by moral crusades, and if the critiques of the AIDS industry are anything to go by, remarkably little has changed in the aftermath of colonial rule.

The aforementioned studies are all explorations of what others have said, fantasized and imagined about African sexuality, rather than of what actually exists. As a result of this focus on perverse colonial and imperial constructions, we still lack an analytical understanding of contemporary sexual relations in Africa's many different societies. This lacuna has been highlighted by the international panic over HIV/AIDS, a hysteria which has revealed the persistence of age-old preoccupations and wholesale ignorance about African sexuality. Now, as in the past, the research that does exist is precipitated by a scourge, and focuses on sexuality as pathogenic.

This leaves a great many areas of African sexual culture unresearched since the early colonial studies of initiation, puberty and marriage rites conducted within the tribal paradigm, or the coffee-table photographic collections of Leni Riefenstal and Mirella Ricardi. Analytical studies of the transformations in the type and form of relationships between the sexes that have accompanied Africa's wide ranging social, economic and political changes are rare, as are studies of masculinity, femininity, heterosexuality, homosexuality, or of the changes wrought by colonisation and decolonization, capitalism, urbanization, militarism, wars, famines or any number of other factors likely to impinge on sexuality.

Genital Mutilation

In view of the political agenda of feminist-inspired research on women and gender relations, it is not surprising to find a number of studies addressing, or attacking, traditions inimical to women. The 1980s saw the publication of several books and reports detailing the various forms of genital mutilation still being carried out in various parts of the region (El Sadaawi 1980, Abdalla 1982, El Dareer 1982, Warsame and Ahmed 1985, Koso-Thomas 1987). It is an area in which scholars have worked hand-in-hand with activist groups to confront the uphill task of organising against deeply-rooted practices that communities are highly sensitive and secretive about. Historically, the colonialists were the first to proscribe and legislate against the misnamed practice of 'female circumcision' in the

1940s and 1950s. As a result of this, opposition to the various forms of genital mutilation became linked with colonial repression. This meant that nationalists as renowned as Kenyatta proclaimed support for clitoridectomy on the basis that it was integral to African tradition and morality, a defensive position which defined progressives who wished to do away with the practice as 'traitors'. Today one can find Westerners as well as Africans being apologists for 'female circumcision', usually insisting that valuable ancient traditions have been misunderstood and misrepresented (e.g. Knudsen 1994 takes this position see below). Against this there is a small but growing pool of empirical research by indigenous as well as international scholars. The damaging and hazardous nature of the various surgical modifications performed on women in different parts of Africa is no longer in question, and justifies the general use of the term 'genital mutilation' to encompass clitoridectomy, various degrees of excision, infibulation, and combinations thereof.

During the last five years, the genital mutilation of women has continued to be a major concern in and beyond the region, and several major books and articles have addressed the topic (e.g. Hicks 1993, Knudsen 1994, SWDO/AIDOS 1989). Of these only one (SWDO/AIDOS 1989) is the product of local activism, and contains the proceedings of a high profile conference organized with the collaboration of the Somali Women's Democratic Organisation (SWDO). The literature is far from comprehensive, and would be greatly enriched and strategically enhanced by a deeper understanding of the material and cultural-ideological conditions under which many of these practices have persisted, or not, as the case may be.

The recent work reflects the continuing concern over the deleterious effects of the various forms of genital mutilation on women and their sexual and reproductive capacities, and tell of some of the efforts to reduce or eradicate the practices (e.g. SWDO/AIDOS 1989). The early tendency to address the issue under the less controversial health policy paradigm has been supplemented by studies which pay greater attention to the cultural dynamics of these practices, particularly the sexual politics underlying them. It is now more widely recognised that the common purpose of female genital mutilation (FGM) is to sustain male control over female sexuality by diminishing women's sexual pleasure. Much has also been made of the fact that in societies where the practice is normalised, some women have vested interests in supporting it.

Perhaps the most ambitious study in recent years is that by Hicks (1993) which focuses on infibulation in Islamic Northeast Africa, where the more extreme forms of excision and infibulation are most pervasive. Deploring the lack of comprehensive and systematic data (even in the Horn of Africa where most of the existing research has taken place) she nonetheless sets out to map the cultural correlates of the practice across 26 infibulating populations and 20 non-infibulating control populations, a sample taken from the 105 groups she identifies in her targeted area (Chad, Ethiopia, Sudan, Somalia and Eritrea).

Unique in its scope, her use of a diachronous statistical analysis leads her to isolate and hierarchically order 21 significantly associated variables, and to identify patterns amongst these, eventually coming up with 8 primary variables and 5 secondary variables which are compositely associated with the practice of infibulation. Of primary relevance are: i) wives retaining full membership in natal group ii) male absenteeism, iii) unstable marriages, iv) low position of women, v) sheep and goats herded by wives, vi) high bride prices, vii) Islam, viii) negative correlation with exogamy. Of secondary relevance are nomadism, a preference for parallel cousin marriage, men being camel and/or cattle owners, and the use of livestock in bride price payments. Although many of the variables she isolates can be found individually in other Moslem pastoral populations, Hicks argues that it is the fact that they are compositely found in infibulating populations which suggests that further studies will reveal their functional importance to the practice.

In her discussion of the composite relationships between these variables, Hicks (1993) observes that 'unstable households' relate to the exigencies of differential mixed herd pasturing, where ecological and domestic instabilities combine to result in lengthy periods of spouse separation, and where a norm of separate sleeping arrangements, perhaps combined with the demands of polygamy, are all likely to lead to psychological distance between husbands and wives.

With regard to Islam, she notes that although Islam has no relationship to the origin and practice of infibulation, it has functioned, and continues to function, as a vehicle for its perpetuation.

It does this by maintaining women's inferior status, alienating them from economic resources and public life, perpetuating modesty codes and physical restriction, symbolically costing them as custodians of male honour, and reasserting men's exclusive rights over female fertility.

Women's weak social position means that the only avenue for social status open to them is through their roles as wives and mothers, a status denied to the uninfibulated. This explains Hicks' remark that in societies where infibulation is practiced, it is incorrect to regard it as a social problem, since it is the uninfibulated that constitute a social problem. Her approach is based on a cultural analysis which recognizes the centrality of infibulation to the lives of women in such societies, and the ostracisation likely to be faced by those who are not subjected to it. As such it marks a change from the sensationalism of many reactions to this custom, and moves away from the medicalisation that has characterised many responses to it.

In her conclusion she discusses the difficulties of effecting change in what she describes as 'closed cultural systems', where infibulation is 'part and parcel of the reproductive process' and the rigid control of women is a direct result of their central role in reproduction. She maintains that the practice cannot therefore be attacked in isolation from the intricate web of social relationships that it is so central to, an insight which suggests that infibulation will not be reduced, let alone eradicated, without profound social transformation. It is this that leads Hicks to argue that in areas where the secularized state has virtually no impact on people's lives or livelihoods, the strategy of using religious authorities to advocate the Sunna circumcision (excision of the clitoris, some of the labia and partial stitching of the wound) over the more drastic pharonic type (cutting out of the clitoris and labia followed by extensive stitching), may be the most effective way to effect change and reduce the appalling consequences of the latter for women's sexual and reproductive capacities. The disadvantage lies in the fact that this is likely to cement the link between Islam and mutilation, a link that has been claimed, but not fully institutionalised to date.

Knudsen (1994) provides a rather less systematic preliminary study of her native Ghana, preferring to use the technically incorrect term 'female circumcision' to avoid appearing judgmental. Why, she wonders, is male circumcision not regarded as a mutilation?[7] Under her preferred heading she addresses a variety of practices, most of which are concerned with the diminution of female sexuality by cutting or scarring of the external genitals. She also mentions the less documented custom of stretching the

---

7   In this authors experiene, male circumcision is regarded as a form of mutilation in communities that do not practice it.

external genitals of women, observing that this too is generally intended to enhance male rather than female sexual pleasure.

However, her study is at its most speculative when she posits a link between 'declining sexual morality' (she names teenage pregnancy) and the demise of these time-honoured customs. She does not remark on the paradoxical fact that Christianity and Islam, both of which impose their own restrictions on sexual freedom, are implicated in the demise of 'female circumcision' in Ghana. It is African traditionalists who perpetrate female genital mutilation (FGM) in Ghana, reaffirming the evidence that these customs are indigenously invented rather than introduced.[8]

From this review we can see that the conditions under which female genitalia are excised, infibulated or otherwise modified differ from place to place. It is interesting that since the demise of colonial rule many such practices appear to have declined in West Africa, whereas, during the same period, they have gained popularity or persisted in many parts of North East Africa. FGM research also suggests that cultural analysis of pre-Islamic and pre-Christian traditions could contribute greatly to our understanding of indigenous gender relations. In view of the constraining effects of FGM on female sexuality, one is left to ask, where is the research on traditions which empower women, which give them more, rayher than less, control of their sexual and reproductive lives? Given the frequent claims to this effect, why is there not more research on aspects of indigenous cultures which empower women sexualilly?

Most other studies in the area of sexuality are linked to one of two major recent international concerns: population growth and HIV\AIDS. It is fair to say that women have most often been researched as perpetrators of both. This material has for the most part been funded by international agencies and directed towards preventative strategies directed at curbing population growth, or curtailing the spread of the HIV/AIDS pandemic. It is not therefore dealt with in this review, beyond noting that the availability of research funding in these areas is leading to a growing number of publications.

---

8   Yoruba tradition has it that the female clitoris will harm or blind a male child during birth, an so practice clitoridectomy.

In addition to this, there are a number of international and African organisations, like the Global Women's Network on Reproductive Health, or the society for women 'AIDS in Africa', which have sought to bring a feminist perspective to bear on these important areas of international policy and intervention, and which have involved African women.

Herstories: Giving Voice to Women

The genre which epitomizes the methodological innovations that have accompanied the development of women's studies is one in which women's voices are given pride of place. It is this methodological commonality which unites studies that cover diverse subject matter. 'Herstories' are best sited under the broad heading of cultural studies because so many of them address women's subjectivity and agency. For this reason they tend to rely on qualitative and in- depth field work which has clear anthropological antecedents. Because of the emphasis on conveying women's consciousness and experience, herstories necessarily embody a holistic approach to women's lives which defies mainstream disciplinary boundaries. Women's accounts of their life experiences and daily practices, their histories and myths, their reflections on their past and present existences: the collection and analysis of these has been one of the major ways through which feminist-inspired scholarship has sought to redress the gender inequities suppressing women's voices and viewpoints. In social science, women's actual social subordination has often been hidden from view, naturalized and compounded by androcentric theoretical frameworks and research methods. Having mounted major epistemological challenges to the imbuement of science with patriarchal values and perceptions, feminist-inspired scholars have made recourse to methods which give women a voice as a way of overcoming their absence from the more conventional archival, library and man-to-man fieldwork sources.

Several different methodological approaches are evident in recent studies of this genre. The first are in-depth, gender sensitive anthropological studies of specific communities of women (e.g. Early 1993), or men and women (Pankhurst 1992). Both of these examples started out with research aims that were abandoned in favour of other aims which seemed more relevant once fieldwork had commenced, something which suggests an intellectual openness and willingness to hear and respond to what women have to say. This responsiveness reflects the influence of a feminist research ethic which demands that research processes be demystified and made, more transparent as well as responsive to the needs and concerns of the women being researched (Roberts 1981, Stanley and Wise 1984, Stanley 1990).

Pankhurst's (1992) book *Gender, Development, and Identity* is more burdened with her own theoretical preoccupations than any of the others, and, although she admits to relying predominantly on biographical interviews with women as her primary source, Pankhurst displays a certain insecurity when she explicitly resists defining her work as being on 'woman and that kind of thing'. The 70 biographical interviews with women that she quotes so extensively in her text were gathered alongside 97 questionnaire interviews mostly with men, use of her own field diaries, and the usual archival and written sources. Her study of the Amharic-speaking village of Gragn in Menz seeks to unravel the relationship between the state and the peasantry in Mengistu's Ethiopia, and to examine gender relations in this context. Yet, lengthy contextualisations and background information notwithstanding, this book is primarily a study of the changes wrought in women's lives by government policy and changing economic conditions, a study which contains rich ethnographic detail, but at the same time provides an analysis of the relationship between the peasant community and Mengistu's state. It illuminates the failure of the state strategy of villagisation, the antagonistic relationship between a militarily powerful and extractive state machinery and the community, and the inefficacious and tokenistic attempts to involve women in administrative and community structures. Pankhurst's research also reveals women's ability to negotiate and manipulate their restricted circumstances in order to attain the least unfavourable of possibilities. Divorce, invariably initiated by women, is identified as a major strategy deployed by women dissatisfied with their situations, with the result that multiple serial marriages are the norm in a society which is unfavourable to women, but which allows them some choices within the overall patriarchal culture.

Early's *Baladi Women of Cairo* (1993) is a study of traditional, urban Egyptian women in the Bulaq Abu'Ala district of Cairo. It is a concentrated documentation of these predominantly low-income women's lives, one which deploys social observation techniques to gather and convey not only the activities, but also the values, wits and multiple identities of Baladi women. A fluent speaker of Arabic, Early spent 3 years observing and gathering material towards the doctoral dissertation which preceded this book acquiring some close friends as well as indispensable informants. Her theoretical concerns are much less cumbersome than Pankhurst's. Although both are anthropologists, and both use what can loosely be termed participant observation methods noting other people's conversations and activities as well as asking questions, Early has none of Pankhurst's ambivalence over relying on women's narratives. She is thus able to convey a much richer and subtler order of information about the realities and concerns of her target group, one which credits them with a greater degree of agency. She concludes not with a tying together of theoretical concerns, but with a summary of what it means to be *baladi*, a meaning that has been developed through her study of the narratives and performances of Baladi women, often through their own counter-position of themselves to the *afrangi* (Westernized, modernized) Egyptians amongst whom they live and work.

At the other end of a continuum in women's studies are compiled biographies and life histories (Mirza and Strobel 1989, Russell 1990, Staunton 1991). Here the researcher's role, is given varying degrees of salience. Russell (1990) is somewhat unjustifiably credited as the 'author' of *Lives of Courage*, a compilation of South African women's stories. Mirza and Strobel (1989) do not claim authorship, but 'edited and translated' life stories of three women of Mombasa, gathered through interviews conducted in Swahili during Strobel's doctoral fieldwork. Staunton (1990), a Zimbabwean does not even put her name to the carefully gathered and presented stories of thirty of her countrywomen's experiences during the liberation war. All three of these collections are written in the first person, retaining the original names and identities of the contributors, and including their photographs. Each woman is thus not only given a space in which to tell her story, but does so in full awareness that she will be appearing in a book for public consumption. They are thus part of the project in a way that is precluded by the conventional use of pseudonyms, a double-edged practice which at once 'protects' and invisibilises the people actually telling the story.

Whereas the majority of the contributors to Staunton's *Mothers of the Revolution* are rural women probably not well known beyond their communities, Russell appears to have made an effort to include many of the famous women active on the South African scene prior to the demise of the apartheid regime, and her book displays accolades from the good and the great (Alice Walker, Nadine Gordimer, Archbishop Desmond Tutu and Oliver Tambo have all been delighted by it). Both Russell's and Staunton's collections revolve on the particular conditions of the respective struggles of the people of South Africa and Zimbabwe, a fact which gives them focus and clarity. Mirza and Strobel (1989) for their part, regard the presentation of three women's lives as informative enough in their own right, and make no explicit attempt to situate them in any given historical or political framework other than that implied by the somewhat diffuse tag of 'Swahiliness'.

The third variation in the women-speak genre combines the commitment to unleashing women's world views and experience with a commitment to reflecting on these, and a recognition of the importance of theorising on the basis of these realities (see Bozzoli 1991, Cock 1992, Macleod 1991). Macleod's book is a rich examination of the lives and strategies of lower-middle class working women in Cairo, whereas the other two are South African studies of women during the apartheid era. All three books are outstanding in their analytical acumen as well as in successfully conveying women's contemporary history. None have any hesitation in asserting the value of listening to what women say, yet neither is this sanctified or assumed to be simple truth. Much attention is given to the social relations of the research process, and the epistemological importance of these.

Bozzoli's authorship of the impressive and politically perceptive book, *Women of Phokeng* includes an acknowledgement of her African fieldworker's contribution: 'with the assistance of Mmantho Nkotsoe'. And so it should. Bozzoli admits that she does not speak or understand the language used by the women of Phokeng, and that as a white woman and an outsider, she would not have been able to attain the intimate level of rapport that Nkotsoe, a university-educated woman from a village neighboring on Phokeng, was able to develop, particularly in view of both the context (under an authoritarian apartheid state) and the subject matter (women's often 'illegal' migrancy). Several pages are devoted to a lengthy exploration of Nkotsoe's relationship with the women of Phokeng, through which all the material was gathered. Bozzoli remarks that the English version of a Setswana original, has to be better than attempting to interview in English, as is still common practice. She implicitly includes herself amongst the 'students of South African society who await the day when a new generation of fluent Bantu-speaking sociologists emerges, *able to convey to the English speaking world* what insights they gain from the analysis of the words of ordinary speakers of their own tongue' (emphasis added) (1991:12).

Bozzoli and Nkotsoe's study uses the oral histories of women born between 1900-1915 to investigate the consciousness, life strategies and movements of women between the so-called homeland of Bophutatswana and the cities. It is the inclusion of the dimension of subjectivity that sets Bozzoli's analysis of these women's lives apart from other studies of life strategy and migration. Whereas the early chapters are devoted to chronologically organized narrative, the later chapters, while retaining the prominence given to women's voices, provide us with a detailed documentation of the process of politicization. It is a process during which women who consider themselves highly respectable find themselves being repeatedly subjected to intimidation and harassment by the authorities, harassment which leads them to develop a counter consciousness that resents and defies the persecutors, thus foretelling the demise of the apartheid regime.

This upholds Bozzoli's thesis that consciousness is organized around life strategies devised by women while it remains linked to, and dependent upon the wider and changing material world in which they live, a world textured by race and gender relations as well as economic forces. The analysis put forward takes us beyond the caricaturized notions of black South Africans, either as victims of apartheid, patriarchy and capitalism, or as heroic revolutionaries. It also transcends the determinism of orthodox materialist analysis, revealing the far more subtle processes through which individual identities are constituted and changed in the course of life, and may be collectivized and politicized, so beginning to resemble ideologies. By conducting her analysis from the bottom up, and by grounding it in the life strategies of her target group, Bozzoli is also able to move beyond the structuralism of grand marxist and early feminist theories, and so make a major theoretical contribution to the study of consciousness.

Cock's (1992) study, Women and War in South Africa is original both in its subject matter and in its methodology. Employing an unstructured interview method rather than the oral history method used in the Bozzoli-Nkotsoe study, Cock bases her analysis of the gender politics of the South African war of liberation on a comparative examination of the experiences of white women within the South African Defence Forces (SADF) and black women in Umkhonto we Sizwe (MK). She begins by noting that both the whites and the Africans come from patriarchal societies lacking any tradition of gender equality, and in a somewhat contentious exercise, likens the apartheid regime, the Congress of South African Trade Unions (COSATU) and the African National Congress (ANC) on the basis that none of them have women playing significant leadership roles.

While the numerical paucity of women in the leadership of all three forums is a matter of empirical fact, her comparison obfuscates the substantial evidence that the ANC and COSATU, while they may be a long way from espousing feminism, have far more progressive gender ideologies than the apartheid state, as any reference to their congresses or the statements made over the years by their leadership would have indicated. Moreover her reference to the diverse African cultures is rather limited, since it is the Zulu culture propounded by Inkatha which she quotes in support of her argument that both African and white cultures, although patriarchal, contain something of a 'tough-but-submissive woman' tradition evident in the images of Voortrekker wives and Zulu mythology respectively.

Several other authors have drawn the comparisons between the gender ideologies of Zulu and Afrikaner nationalism, but these have stopped short of suggesting that the African liberation movement and the apartheid regime shared more than the most superficial similarities in gender politics (Gaitskell and Unterhalter 1989, Hassim 1993, McClintock 1995). The interview excerpts reveal a far more subtle complex of gender values and attitudes than is suggested by the rather global analysis of South African gender politics which Cock puts forward as a prelude to her commendable study of the role of women in the armed forces of the apartheid regime and in the struggle against it. Here more space is devoted to the highly conventional gender dynamics of the South Africa Defence Force (SADF) than to those of 'the resisters': MK and the End Conscription Campaign (ECC). The picture that emerges of SADF is one of a conventional military organisation with highly circumscribed gender roles, which relies on notions of men as 'protectors' of women, and which cannot therefore countenance more equal participation of women. The increased participation of white women in SADF in recent years is attributed to the exigencies of being a losing side, rather than any radical change. The interview material reveals something of the motivations of white women entering SADF: many of them are simply seeking a training ground or a short career prior to marriage, rather than having clear ideological commitments for or against the regime they serve. It is on this point that they differ from the MK women who come across as being politically aware, committed to the liberation struggle and highly motivated, as indeed must be the case for any person (male or female) volunteering to undertake training as a guerrilla, and thereafter to participate in actions against the powerful military machine of the apartheid state. Neither SADF nor MK deploy women in combat roles, although perhaps because MK are ideologically committed to gender equality they do give women the same training (including the use of weapons and explosives) as men.

Cock's consideration is fascinating but brief: a more detailed study of women in the pre- and post-apartheid military forces remains very much in order. Her material is used to reconsider the confrontation between feminism and militarism that has been in evidence since Wollestonecraft first argued for women to take an anti-militarist position. A great many feminists have concurred with the conventional view that war is 'men's business', and that women should have nought to do with military matters. As Cock observes, this persistent view is not one which has been espoused by many Third World feminists. For many of us, participation in armed struggles has often been a necessary aspect of the national liberation movement, colonial legacies and military traditions of sexism notwithstanding. African revolutionary movements have (justifiably or unjustifiably) prided themselves on their inclusion of women (see Urdang 1989 on Mozambique's Frelimo, Wilson 1991 on Eritrea's EPLF). Feminists remain divided into those who feel that equality means equal participation in the violence as well as the glories of war, and those who feel that women should stay out of this unpalatable aspect of human endeavour. Both schools of thought ultimately seek to build a world in which wars do not occur: the question is whether this can best be done by entering the powerful military establishment and participating in military activities, or remaining outside it, a question which Cock poses and explores through her material but, perhaps wisely, does not answer definitively.

Macleod's (1991) *Accommodating Protest* shares the methodological commitments of Bozzoli and Cock. Like Early (1993) she has the advantage of being able to speak the mother tongue of her target group. She too is able to develop intimate relationships with women in the community she has targeted, and over a period of time, gathers oral data comprising narrative about various aspects of their lives (discussed in more detail above under 'Women, Religion, Resistance'). Her central interest is in exploring women's subjectivity and agency, to develop a theoretical understanding of women's apparent willingness to conform to patriarchal hegemony.

What distinguishes all these studies is the degree to which women's agency is revealed, something only possible through the open-ended, woman-centred methods that all of them deploy. It is a paradigm which takes the study of the oppression that all these women experience far beyond the earlier, granded theoretical frameworks, which often failed to convey the subtleties, nuances and innovations that make women makers of history rather than mere victims of it.

Work and Economy

Conceptual Issues

Studies of women's work have led to major reconceptualisations of what we mean by the terms 'work' and 'economy'. The fact that men and women perform different tasks in most societies has led scholars interested in gender to study the sexual division of labour. To say that there is a sexual division of labour means that not only do men and women perform different kinds of work, but that their labour is also differentially valued and remunerated in accordance with the gender of the workforce performing it.

A separate but related issue is the invisibilisation of women's work. It has long been apparent that a substantial amount of the work that women perform in most parts of the world has not been included in the formal definitions of 'work' or 'labour', because these have generally referred to waged employment in a formal economy in which men have predominated. Many of the tasks carried out by women in and beyond the household have thus been taken for granted, rendered invisible and devalued. The most obvious jobs included here are housework, child-bearing and child-care and food preparation, but in many contexts 'domestic' labour has also included small-scale farming and household-level production of both food and goods for the market.

In capitalist economies, work has been unjustly divided into productive and reproductive spheres, with production defined in economistic terms denoting production of tradable goods and expropriatable surplus. Work concerned with biological and social reproduction has not been included in most macroeconomic calculations, except where these have been performed as waged work. For the most part such work is still not considered, or if carried out as waged work, is so devalued that it is poorly paid. In short much of what has tended to be defined as 'women's work' has been unpaid, whatever its centrality to the functioning of the formal labour force, and indeed, of the society as a whole. This unequal scenario has been facilitated by gender ideologies which convey notions of maternal altruism, of wifely duty, and of men's right to women's service and nurturance, and to control their reproductive capacities.

Whether this has always been the case in all societies has been the subject of much historical and anthropological study and speculation. Historical and cross-cultural studies have revealed that the sexual division of labour prevailing in Western capitalist societies is far from universal. Even here, it has changed radically over the generations, influenced by the advent of wars, economic booms and slumps and other macro-economic phenomena. Nonetheless, at the ideological level, notions of what women should and can do have been unreasonably consistent: women's work has invariably included the unpaid labour of housework, childbearing, cooking and caring for children, husbands and other relatives, and a plethora of other domestic and reproductive tasks. In bourgeois capitalist societies these are performed in increasingly atomised individual households, consumer units headed by male authority figures who, for their part, are supposed to be the economic providers.

Empirical studies show this scheme to be a patriarchal fantasy which has seldom been attained by the majority of households. Even within the West, poorer families have seldom been able to rely on a single income, and a great many families do not conform to the idealised man-woman-and-two-point-four-children model. The nuclear family is even less of an option in other parts of the world, however much it has been extolled. Migration patterns, forced labour, economic exigencies, extended family patterns, polygamy and other customs are just some of the factors militating against wholesale embracement of the hegemonic family type. Nonetheless, because the ideological currency of the male-headed nuclear unit has been so powerful, women in many parts of the world perform a great many unremunerated tasks, regardless of whether or not men are providing for them. Discussions of women's work cannot escape acknowledging the pervasive influence of this pernicious familial ideology in creating an unequal sexual division of labour that impinges on all aspects of women's labour.

African research into gender relations and work is particularly fascinating because of the enormous range of activities that African women engage in and the permutations that these have undergone with the changing circumstances of pre-colonial, colonial and post-colonial societies. Here we see that the sexual divisions of labour have been subjected to such major transformations that any notions of the immutability of what men and women can or should do are rendered nonsensical. Furthermore, consideration of the activities that women engage in subvert many of the dichotomies that have been developed to characterise labour, notably those between formal and informal work, between productive and reproductive work, and between the household and the market.

Above and beyond all this, the African research into gender relations reveals the remarkable creativity with which African women, widely perceived as beasts of burden hopelessly locked into their exploitation, have addressed their situation, negotiated new terms in their relationships both with individual men and with governments, and have come up with innovative ways of ensuring the economic survival, not only of themselves, but of entire families and communities.

Women's Work in Pre-colonial Africa

Little of the recent gender research carried out on Africa has addressed work in the pre-colonial period in its own right. Set against the burgeoning literature on labour relations in the colonial period, the few available studies suggest a great deal more than they state. Most of the insights contained therein derive from observations about the impact of colonisation, often gathered from archives and records, journals and travelogues, and from oral histories obtained from those old enough to recollect what things were like before the white man came. Historical studies have been supplemented by research carried out in remote communities where the impact of colonialism is thought to have been less directly felt, and more of the 'old ways' are thought to have survived. Both the gender bias in existing material, and the tendency for the past to be romanticized and idealised pose substantial methodological challenges which newer and more gender-aware research is now taking greater cognizance of.

Schmidt's (1992) study of Shona women in Zimbabwean history devotes her first two chapters to a discussion of gender relations on the eve of colonial conquest, detailing the various activities women and men engage in traditional society, and how these related to their social and political status. Nineteenth century Shona society is characterised as having been unrelentingly patriarchal, with women having no direct voice in public affairs and no control over social resources:

> male chiefs, headmen and other elders made the decisions that governed public life, regulating relations and settling disputes...Senior men controlled the distribution of such crucial resources as land and wives, thus monopolizing control over the society's reproductive capacity. They exercised authority over the labour power of women, children, and junior men, and wielded institutionalized religious and political power (Schmidt 1992:14).

With rare exceptions, it seems that women only achieved status by bearing children for the male lineage into which they were married. They were subject to the complete authority of their in-laws, for whom they were expected to labour on the land and in the household. Since polygamy was widely practiced, junior wives were also subject to senior wives. On widowhood, women were inherited by their late husband's nearest male relative. Even less fortunate were those women who were captured as slaves by rival groups, or pawned by male relatives in times of economic hardship. Yet others were held as hostages or exchanged in the settlement of disputes. In all such cases, women were subject to the full authority of the men they had been pawned to or captured by, and were expected to work for and provide such sexual services as might be required. Such relationships could culminate in marriage, and in the case of women held as pawns, *lobola* (dowry) would then be paid to the woman's kin, or some portion of the debt relieved by the creditor-suitor.

In what was primarily an agricultural society, Shona women carried out the bulk of agricultural labour on their husbands' family land. Production of food and children were their two most important responsibilities, but both were conducted under the full control of their spouses. Women also engaged in the gathering of wild fruit, vegetables and insects for domestic consumption. What women did control was the produce of their own small plots, and any gifts accruing from their successful bearing of children. Women fetched wood and water, pounded maize, ground millet and prepared food. Schmidt's account suggests that men's participation in agriculture, while not as consistent or gruelling as women's, was nonetheless crucial. They were primarily responsible for cattle rearing, and undertook seasonal agricultural tasks, particularly bush clearing and crop threshing.

Furthermore, activities such as harvesting and guarding ripening crops were shared, often being carried out by family parties of men, women and children. Hunting too is described as involving parties of men, women and children. Armed men and boys protected herds and performed various other specialized tasks including weaving and clothes production, carving, ceramic production, mining and iron smelting, building the framework and thatching the roofs of houses and granaries. Both sexes participated in seasonal gold mining, with women doing most of the panning and washing the alluvial. In short, life in pre-colonial Shona society involved a great deal of work for both sexes, but arrogated to men all authority, the ownership of most property, and control over the land and the labour of women and children.

Guy's (1990) more general review of gender relations in precapitalist southern African societies attempts to delineate common features, many of which hold true for the Shona society described by Schmidt (1992). Like Schmidt, Guy characterizes gender oppression as endemic to Southern African societies. Instead of entering into the debate over whether women were better or worse off prior to the capitalist penetration that accompanied colonisation than after it, he emphasizes the differences between precapitalist and capitalist forms of gender exploitation. Land productivity, cattle, and women's fertility were important for the survival and continuation of pre-colonial communities. Guy (1990) argues that marriage was a major means of ensuring exchange of cattle as well as both land productivity (through women's labour) and reproduction of the labour force (through childbearing) and this ensured the value of women, so securing for them a central social position not so evident in capitalist societies.

Kapteijns (1994) reaches a similar conclusion with regard to Somali women, whom she argues, have lost their traditional status as bearers of a complex set of reciprocal rights and duties in the rural, predominantly nomadic culture that existed prior to colonial and capitalist penetration. According to her analysis, rural patriarchy, oppressive though it may have been, contained certain guarantees for women. The development of urban life and capitalist patriarchy has exchanged certainty for uncertainty, while providing very few new options for women who are now left to operate with little of the protection afforded to women in the more rigid pre-colonial system. She does not take her argument beyond this to consider the possibility that the breakdown of rural patriarchy might offer more options to women in the long term.

As a prelude to her discussion of women's central contribution to cash crop production in colonial Ghana, Grier (1992) provides us with a detailed discussion of gender and class relations in pre-colonial Akan society. In contrast to the southern and eastern African patrilineal societies discussed above, Akan society is matrilineal, and so might erroneously have been expected to be less oppressive to women. However, her depiction makes it clear that Akan society was not matriarchal, since authority and power remained vested in men, the main difference being that it lay with maternal uncles instead of fathers and husbands. Relations between men and their wives varied according to the type of marriage contract, often being affected by the coexisting systems of pawnship and slavery. A man married to a woman did not exercise full authority over her labour or responsibility for their offspring unless he married a slave woman. A man married to a freeborn woman could however enhance his authority over her if her uncles fell into debt, thereby enabling him to take her as his pawn. Only then could he claim exclusive rights to her sexuality, the right to half of any wealth she accumulated, and exercise full control over her labour. Grier's (1992:313) account of Akan social relations, depicts a society in which although gender relations varied with caste and status,

> all women were 'perpetual jural minors': no matter what their age, individual wealth, or descent, they fell under the legal guardianship of a male. Their situation contrasted sharply to that of freeborn men. Freeborn men moved from one 'class' to another in their lifetime, whereas freeborn women did not.

Under these circumstances, while some women could and did accumulate some wealth or land, their ability to command the labour of others was severely constrained, and this constituted a major obstacle to their accumulation and development. More likely than not, women were bound to labour for others and unable to reap the benefits of their toil.

This discussion takes us into the colonial period, during which we see that sub-regional differences were at times augmented and at times diminished by the impact of colonial capitalism as it took different forms in the different reaches of the continent.

Labour Relations during Colonialism

Colonial capitalism interacted highly selectively with the diverse indigenous systems, to generate concrete new sexual divisions of labour which altered, but did not remove, the exploitation of women in the household, the community and the labour market. That colonialism transformed African labour and gender relations has long been established. Recent research has concentrated on documenting the specifics of what happened when and where in more detail. We now have a growing body of richly informative studies of gender and labour in colonial times. Issues of colonial gender and labour relations are also frequently addressed in works which are not purely labour studies (e.g. White's 1990 study of prostitution in colonial Nairobi, Bozzoli's 1991 study of Phokeng women) or which address particular groups of women (e.g. Schmidts study of Shona women). Journal articles and book chapters also contain information about women and work during colonialism across a scattering of countries in the rest of the region (see below). There are however, many areas that have not been studied at all, so that there is great scope for researchers interested in gender and labour studies in much of Africa.

Women and Waged Work in Colonial Africa

The domestication of African women has been a recurring theme in studies of gender relations during the colonial period, and it is one which is central to the analysis of the changes in the sexual division of labour that accompanied the colonial incursion and the penetration of capitalism (see chapters by Cock, Meintjes, Hughes & Gaitskell, all in Walker ed. 1990; Ch. 2 in Berger 1992; Ch. 5 in Schmidt 1992; chapters by Hunt, Musisi and Denzer in Hansen 1992). This literature tells us that the ideology of domesticity has provided the rationale and the justification for the exclusion of women from many areas of the paid labour force and the invisibilisation of women's work outside of it. It has also enabled the under-remuneration of those women working in the wage economy. The fact that women have been lured into bearing many of the social costs of production looking after the sustenance, health and welfare of male workers and producing future generations of workers so that these can be left out of economic equations, has also facilitated the exploitation of male labour. While the European origin of a feminine ideal which limits women to the role of a dependent housewife and mother has been emphasised, recent studies also highlight the resonance between this and the desires of men raised in African patriarchal cultures which also render women subordinate to the men in their lives (e.g. Mack 1992).

The employment of women as paid domestic workers has also been the subject of much attention since Cock's (1989) germinal South African study Maids and Madams. In contexts where the ideology of domesticity ensured the exclusion of women from most forms of waged employment, this was often one of the few options for women seeking jobs.

Berger's (1992) study although primarily concerned with women in industry, contains much information on domestic labour. According to her, South African women found waged work as domestics long before they entered the factories, but this was not out of choice. She present evidence that all races of women resisted entering domestic servitude because of the low pay, the demeaning and tedious character of the work and the vulnerability and isolation of women working in private homes. Even here, employers preferred to use poor white women, either from Afrikaner families or recruited from England, so that it was only when these became increasingly unavailable that black women began to be employed in domestic service, despite reluctance from both African and white quarters. Because African women were loath to become servants, and white women feared that their husbands would engage in sexual relations with female servants, male 'houseboys' predominated at the beginning of the century, particularly in the Transvaal and Natal. In the Cape however, women were incorporated into colonial society as domestics much earlier than elsewhere in the region (Berger 1992, Cock 1990).

Cock (1990) notes that during the 1820s many Xhosa women were taken as captives and effectively enslaved in white households. Subsequently, following the encroachments of white settlers, a great many more found themselves displaced and their communities destroyed, and so had little option but to voluntarily enter domestic service. Cock (1990) elucidates the role that missionaries played in the incorporation of Xhosa women into colonial society. Evangelists, motivated by their abhorrence of the customs of *lobola*, polygamy and initiation rites and their desire to secure male converts, took it upon themselves to 'liberate' Xhosa women. As early as 1871, industrial schools began introducing programmes to prepare African women for work as domestics or seamstresses.

Schmidt's (1992) discussion of domestic service in what was then Southern Rhodesia also highlights missionary activity. The practice of sheltering runaways provided a steady flow of women converts, most of whom were able to obtain a minimal education designed to prepare them for domestic service, either as servants or as the wives of male converts. She points out that both African men and white women lobbied against even this circumscribed form of waged employment, each for their own reasons: African men resented the loss of control over women who left rural homesteads for mission compounds, while white women lived in fear of their husbands sexual interest in black women. It was this that motivated the Women's League to campaign for a law proscribing sex between white men and African women (sex between African men and white women already carried heavy penalties for the men concerned). The unwillingness of white women to perform menial domestic tasks themselves combined with a number of other colonial interests to ensure that, in contrast to the situation in neighboring South Africa, and despite the periodic labour shortages that Southern Rhodesia experienced, African men were often employed to work as domestics in European homes (Schmidt 1992 Ch. 6). Hansen's (1992) study of Lusaka indicates that the same was true of Zambia.

West African material pays less attention to the domestic servitude of women because, albeit for a different set of reasons, here too African men were most commonly employed as domestic workers throughout the colonial period. This is at least partly a consequence of the fact that the colonisation of West Africa was carried out predominantly by men. As much for health and climatic reasons as for economic and political ones, West Africa was not subjected to any significant degree of white settlement. Instead the colonial enterprise was carried out by a much smaller number of male administrators who established close collaboration with existing (or appointed) indigenous rulers. White women remained a somewhat unwelcome rarity in these colonies, but here too 'miscegenation' taboos meant that it was regarded as unseemly for European men to employ African women in their homes. The result was that domestic labour was carried out by menservants known as 'houseboys', 'small boys', cooks and gardeners. In any case, in Muslim areas like Northern Nigeria, it was inconceivable that local women would undertake domestic service in the homes of unbelievers. Elsewhere, West African women were too indispensable to their own communities, being required to perform agricultural and economic, as well as domestic, activities.

Throughout the colonial period, African women were almost completely excluded from all other areas of waged employment. The few available studies of women's employment in colonial government service indicate that this was so limited and constrained by imperial gender ideologies that it was only after independence that significant numbers of women began to be employed by African governments (on Ghana see Perbi 1992, on Nigeria see Denzer 1989). Even then, the patterns of gender discrimination were to prove resistant to change and discriminatory legislation persisted.

The colonial state engendered a range of laws and policies which excluded women from waged work, both in government (Perbi 1992, Denzer 1989) and in industry (Berger 1992). As public opinion moved in favour of allowing women to undertake at least some jobs, the tone of the ideological justifications precluding gender equality became increasingly couched in the language of protection. Protectionism proved to be a double-edged sword, on the one hand preventing excessive exploitation of 'vulnerable' women by employers, but on the other hand invoking conservative notions of femininity which prevented women from gaining access to some of the more lucrative and highly paid areas of work. During the colonial period, as since, protectionist legislation has been based on concern over women's reproductive capacities and familial responsibilities, for example precluding women from overtime, night work and physically arduous tasks.

The exclusion of women from the formal waged economy is clearly related to the ideology of domesticity discussed above. The fact that it was primarily men who were coerced, cajoled and taxed into taking up waged employment in the colonial economy did not mean that women in any way escaped both direct and indirect consequences of advancing capitalist exploitation. The situation has varied widely across the region, but it is increasingly possible to discern sub-regional patterns in the gendered organisation of work during the colonial period.

In southern Africa the general scenario that emerges is one in which men migrated to urban areas and mining compounds to take up waged work, leaving women to continue food crop farming and raise children and provide for their in laws and the elderly in the rural areas. In this way, the colonial economy was able to extract male labour, while bearing none of the costs of its welfare or reproduction. Accommodation in hostels and barracks was most often provided for single male workers only, suggesting that their families were expected if not ordained to remain in the rural homesteads, where they might be visited. The 'male breadwinner' was not however paid enough to fully support his family, with the result that family survival came to rely increasingly on labour of women in food production and whatever informal activities proved tenable in a given area. African women did not find their situation improved by having an absentee wage-earning husband, since they found themselves deprived of their co-workers on the family land. Their existing workloads were thus amplified, women who stayed behind having little option other than to take on many of the tasks that would traditionally have been the responsibility of their husbands. Furthermore, as Africans were increasingly dispossessed of the lands they had farmed for generations, and the whole balance of the economy changed, the conditions under which rural women laboured often worsened. Economic support from waged husbands was often intermittent at best, and in any case, the wages paid to African men were seldom high enough to maintain dependants or to compensate for the loss of male labour.

Beale's (1990) study of the employment situation of Indian women under indentureship in Natal (1860-1911) illustrates that women faced direct capitalist exploitation (see above). Despite their being largely excluded from formal waged employment, once employers discovered they could extract women's (or even children's) labour at even lower cost than that paid for African men's labour, they did not hesitate to do so. Because women were not really viewed as 'workers', the employment of women was not subject to even the minimal controls and conditions regulating the employment of men. As a result they could be used in casual and indirect ways that were less secure and more poorly paid than that of men. Indian women were imported to South Africa, not because there was work for them, but perforce, as a result of the Indian governments insistence on a 29 per cent quota of women accompanying every shipload of male workers. Entering a policy vacuum, Indian women had none of the minimal rights to food or housing afforded to their compatriots. They were found themselves at the mercy of both unscrupulous employers and countrymen imbued with contempt for women living outside the strictures of the patriarchal family, caste and class arrangements with which they were familiar. Once the employers discovered the pool of near-destitute Indian women and children, both became used as cheap, disposable labour, to carry out seasonal work on demand, with no further obligations incumbent on the employer. So it was that many Indian women found themselves working 11-13 hour days on tea estates, sorting on the coal faces and occasionally labouring as domestic servants. Those whose husbands did not earn enough to feed them accompanied unmarried women, divorcees and widows to work under the appalling conditions which offered the only alternative to starvation and homelessness, or the most desperate forms of prostitution in the male dormitories of the mine compounds and estate barracks.

African women have been altogether prevented from obtaining waged work for much of South Africa's history. Only in the inter-war years were they allowed into bottom-level factory work when the non-availability of sufficient numbers of white women or African men and economic constraints forced employers to find a cheaper alternative. Here protectionist legislation combined gender concerns with racist rationales. Berger (1992) tells us that in 1930s South Africa there was a vocal campaign to prohibit white women from working under the supervision of black (usually Asian) men (Berger 1992:82). During this period, the South Africans extended protectionism beyond the workplace, into the regulation of women workers accommodation and leisure activities in the form of hostels, initially for white 'working girls'.

A great deal of Berger's book is devoted to the history of white women in South African industry. Her study demonstrates that the situation of the majority of white 'working girls' was unenviable. Employed in significant numbers as industrial workers, from the 1920s on, the prevailing gender ideology saw to it that wage levels were kept extremely low. Women workers, the majority of whom were unmarried, were expected to live as dependants of their families, and to be working for 'a little extra' rather than for a living wage.

In west Africa a somewhat different picture emerges. Although male migration did occur in some instances, it was nowhere as pervasive as it was in southern and eastern Africa. The absence of large scale white settlement also produced major differences in the type and form of colonisation. White and African farmers were not in direct competition for land and markets, rather it was a case of the smaller numbers of Europeans finding ways of getting African peasant farmers to produce the crops required for the international market in the most cost effective way. This most often meant replacing smallholder food production with cash crop production. Here too, small holder food production was continued by women and poorer men, while those men who could go into the farming of cocoa, coffee, palm-nut, rubber and groundnut did so. In so doing they continued to utilize the unpaid labour of their wives and children so that this subsidized the production costs.

The literature on waged labour and gender in the colonial period indicates that the ideology of domesticity and the concomitant exclusion of African women from waged work has had profound consequences on the exploitation of labour as a whole, consequences which served colonial interests and unrelentingly undermined the economic position, not only of women, but of men as well.

Research attention to the exclusion of women from the formal sector has tended to emphasise the role of the colonialists, but the evidence that is presented suggests that African men had their own reasons for not favouring the employment of women in waged jobs that became increasingly sought after. Thus it was not entirely fictitious for Europeans to insist that African men would never accept women in their workplaces, and they were able to use this to justify discriminatory policies and practices which actually furthered their own ends, to the detriment of African workers.

Colonial Informal Sector

African women did not simply accept the situation they faced, either in the declining rural homesteads and smallholdings, or as super-exploited workers. Eastern and southern African research in particular has begun to address the fact that large numbers of women migrated to the towns and across borders, which were after all, imposed on them by the Europeans. They left the homesteads in droves, either to accompany migrant men, or in their own right electing to move away from the controls and circumscriptions of life with their in-laws and elders under deteriorating rural conditions.

Bozzoli (1991) is a path-breaking study of women's migration to work in South Africa[9] (see also Walker 1990, Bonner 1990). White's (1990) study of prostitution in colonial Nairobi is also seminal, and provides numerous rich insights into the lives of women who independently or otherwise moved to Nairobi and, on finding no place for themselves in the labour market, made careers for themselves selling sexual services. Because they displayed great initiative and entrepreneurialism, a number managed to accumulate property and wealth. This leads White to characterise Nairobi's sex workers as 'urban pioneers' who were often well respected in the African communities where they lived. Her celebratory stance towards a generally stigmatized group has led some to accuse her of glamourising African prostitution, and of propagating the notion that this has been the only route to social mobility available to African women (see Zeleza's 1993 review). It is true that White seeks to redress the negative image of prostitutes which has often provided a rationale for the harassment and brutalization of women in African towns by both colonial and post-colonial regimes, and that she has chosen to focus on prostitution rather than on, say, petty trading, beer brewing or nursing. However, it is the focus on sex work that makes it an original and important study which, by bringing a subaltern group under the analytical lens, casts new light on the social character of the colonial towns.

Both of these studies tell us that in the urban areas, and excluded from virtually all forms of waged work, women migrants found numerous ways of earning their living in what was to become known as the informal sector. They took up beer brewing, food preparation, laundering, and the provision of the numerous domestic, social and other services needed by male workers living singly in hostels or compounds lacking in amenities. In these

---

9   After a somewhat complicated history, the Union of South Africa was formed in 1910, and South Africa cannot therefore be regarded as a colony in the same sense as other African countries, since African people were dominated by south African white settlers rather than European nationals.

activities African women found work that required no additional training, since they were able to earn a living from the very tasks that they had been duty bound to perform as wives, mothers and daughters. Brewing and the provision of sexual services have attracted the most attention, both from the colonial authorities and in the literature on the period, a fact which makes it worth reiterating that despite the lucrative nature of these two activities, African women have undertaken many other forms of work besides these.

Trading, mostly small-scale buying and selling, is probably the most widespread income-generating activity not only in West Africa, but also in the eastern and southern parts of the continent, while both women and girls have been involved in the preparation and selling of food, as well as in growing food and transporting it to the towns for sale. Schmidt's (1992) includes several chapters on the agricultural and trading activities of Shona women in colonial Zimbabwe.

In the rural areas too, women engaged in informal activities, as a means of obtaining cash, not just in casual and subsistence agricultural production, but also in trading, basket and cloth weaving, bead-making and the small-scale production of ceramics, numerous items for sale in local and subsequently for tourist markets.

To sum up the literature on women's work during the colonial period, it seems fair to say that imported and local gender ideologies militated against women gaining much foothold in the colonial labour market and economy. Women were largely left out of the colonial design, or kept under the control of men to facilitate the exploitation of labour, in the interlinked reproductive and productive domains. One result of this exclusion was the emergence of an urban informal sector, in which women were (and continue to be) disproportionately represented in activities which conform to their decreed feminine roles as providers of food, care and nurturance to men, but which now became commoditised. Severely limited access to Western-type education prevented women from obtaining skills other than those ordained by Western notions of femininity, thus ensuring their marginalisation in an expanding labour market that was at first exclusively male, and subsequently dominated by men.

One consequence of this was that African women were not proletarianized. They are correspondingly poorly represented in the history of labour struggles during the colonial period. The vast majority remained unproletarianized, working in atomised and individualistic ways to eke out a living for themselves and their dependants under extremely unfavourable conditions. Nonetheless, even the scanty references to women in the labour studies literature do suggest that they often supported men's struggles, providing food and morale-boosting to striking miners and industrial workers, since they too had a stake in men obtaining better wages and conditions. Once they did enter the industrial wage-earning sector, women also began to participate in and initiate strikes and industrial action, so engaging in struggle to improve their conditions (Berger 1992, Mashinini 1989).

Contemporary Situation

The achievement of self-government has not by and large resulted in revolutionary changes in the gender division of labour. This is not to say that there have not been any changes at all, but that, by and large, gender inequalities have persisted. Perhaps the most dramatic change that has followed independence is the increase in the numbers of both men and women receiving formal education, and thus becoming available for formal sector employment. In the early years it became for some a matter of national pride to have women in highly-placed positions, as was the case when Nkrumah appointed three women ministers to his cabinet in 1958. This liberal spirit was accompanied by a lifting of some of the restrictions that colonial governments had imposed on women's employment in the public sector.

The formal waged sector of the labour market has never been very large in most African countries. In recent times there is also a general contraction in both the public and private formal sector, brought about by the imposition of structural adjustment policies. This has created an overall trend towards informalisation, with its own gender implications. Nonetheless, it is still true to say that the women have been disproportionately under-represented in the formal sector in all African countries. This under-representation is even more pronounced at higher salary levels, and applies to both public and private sector employment. The vast majority of African women have remained in the vulnerable and less organized realm of informal and self-employment, with only a minority attaining enough education and training to break the patterns laid down in the colonial period.

It is therefore not surprising to find that research attention has focused on African women's informal activities, to the neglect of their numerically small but significant contribution to the formal sector. The nature of this contribution is most evident in studies of government and public services, also the most significant because of their role in labour policy formulation, and their impact on the wider society through their administrative and regulatory roles. Since the institution of structural adjustment programmes (SAP) during the 1980s, cutbacks in civil and public services have undermined the status of government as the major formal sector employer, with as yet unexamined effects on the employment of women therein. Have cutbacks led to women and other vulnerable groups being laid off proportionately more than men? Or have low real wage levels, combined with the declining importance of government, led men to make their exit into more lucrative private sector jobs, so leaving spaces to be filled by women seeking greater job security? What have the implications of such changes had for the informal sector, and the gender differences therein?

These and a great many questions have not yet been substantively addressed in studies of gender and work in the contemporary period. Instead, researchers have concentrated on the roles of African women as traders, subsistence farmers and urban entrepreneurs, a focus which, although numerically justifiable, does not present a complete picture of African women's work and their changing position in the labour market (see e.g. Adepoju and Oppong 1994).

The Formal Sector

The increased participation of women in formal sector employment since independence has not, by and large, challenged the gender conservatism that characterised the colonial period. Women have taken up work as industrial workers, nurses, teachers, agricultural workers, professional cleaners, caterers, typists, with smaller but still significant numbers entering the professions of medicine, law, banking, business, management, academia, and various aspects of civil and public service. Despite these overall increases, gender differences in both educational levels and in formal employment have proved remarkably persistent, with men far outnumbering women in all but a few select areas. These areas are those which conform to colonial notions of femininity: catering, cleaning, secretarial work, teaching and nursing.

Detailed studies of the processes through which women have entered the formal sector in some areas but not others, and the organizational dynamics that have kept women particularly underrepresented in senior positions across the board are few and far between. Notable exceptions are afforded by the studies of Berger (1992) whose seminal book on women in South African industry contains several chapters on the contemporary period, and

Marks (1994), who carried out a detailed study of the nursing profession as a microcosm of the sex and race politics of apartheid. The fact that both are South African studies may have something to do with the fact that it is in this highly industrialised economy that women constitute a significant proportion of the urban proletariat. One third of the formal workforce in South Africa are women, the highest figure for the entire region.

Recent years have yielded astonishingly few publications specifically addressing women's participation in the formal labour market in the rest of the region, although the subject of women's work does feature in ethnographic and oral history studies of women's lives. Macleod 1991, for example, contains detailed discussion of women's increasing uptake of lower-middle level waged jobs in Cairo over the last few years. The searches that were carried out did not locate any academic studies addressing the role of women in the formal private sector.

In the public sector, sexual discrimination continues to thrive in various guises, legislation and policy pronouncements notwithstanding (e.g. Akuffo 1990, Kieh and Railey 1993, Badri 1991).

The centrality of the public sector, both as the site at which employment policies are made and where all aspects of national decision-making and planning takes place is worth emphasizing. Given the weakness and marginality of the informal sector and the powerlessness of those engaged in unpaid work, it is the formal sector that must be targeted if there are to be any significant changes in the sexual division of labour.

The data available on Ghana is probably suggestive of a wider regional situation (Ardayfio-Schandorf 1990, Akuffo 1990). Here the picture is one in which there has been a dramatic change since independence, but overall it is a case of so far, but no further. There are currently a small number of women in senior Government positions: 2 sit on the advisory council of state, there are 3 full Ministers (as was the case in Nkrumah's first cabinet) 16 are Directors in the Civil Service and a small number are Chairpersons of Public Boards and Corporations (own fieldwork 1995). Despite the growing numbers of qualified professional women (in medicine, law, accounting and engineering numbering 3.4 per cent of the female workforce in 1984), there are still very few occupying senior managerial or decision-making positions (0.1 per cent of the female workforce in 1984).

The majority of women in the public and civil services are employed at the lowest levels as typists and stenographers, telephonists, salesgirls, caterers and cleaners. Middle level women are mostly junior administrators, bank cashiers, teachers (concentrated in nursery and primary schools and fewer in secondary schools and nurses (data cited in Ardayfio-Schandorf 1990). Both Akuffo (1990) and Ardayfio-Schandorf (1990) identify unequal access to education as the major obstacle to women's advancement, but Akuffo also draws attention to institutionalised patterns of discrimination: in language, in access to medical care, housing, funeral grants and allowances and in access to training and promotion opportunities. Yet women constitute only 9.3 per cent of union membership and are seldom active in agitation for better or fairer conditions.

In East Africa, Hollway and Mukurasi (1991) carried out a case study of obstacles to women's promotion in the Tanzanian civil service, looking at both the formal and informal workings of the organisation in what has been a relatively favourable post-independence environment for women. Following Mukurasi's (1991) autobiographical account of discrimination, this study revealed a pattern similar to that uncovered by the Ghanaian studies cited above: one in which many women are active and dedicated employees, but very few are able to attain senior positions, despite the legislation affirming women's equality. Being an in-depth study, Hollway and Mukurasi (1991) were able to identify some of the organizational dynamics perpetuating this situation in a way that few other studies have.

Badri (1991) looks at women in management and public administration in the Sudan, noting the great increase in women's entry into government service where they constituted as many as 40 per cent of government employees in 1981. She is unable to present figures on the proportion of women attaining managerial positions, but instead compares data about women who are managers from three studies. Her findings indicate that women managers are generally highly qualified, ambitious and highly motivated, but that their employers have somewhat less faith in their capacities, and emphasize the encumbrances placed on married women by their primary obligations to domestic duties.

All three authors concur in acknowledging the effect of women's 'double burden' on their career advancement, drawing attention to the lack of support for mothers of young children, and the fact that women continue to bear the full domestic burden. On the other hand it appears that while many women are taxed by their multiple responsibilities, there is no evidence that they actually perform any less efficiently as a result of them, although this is what many employers believe. None of the studies go so far as to suggest that for the public sector to become more equal, it might also be necessary for the gender relations in the domestic realm to undergo change to accommodate the greater responsibilities of women working outside the home. This would require either greater participation of men in childbearing and domestic work, or the employment of others to do so, whether this is done individually in private homes or collectively through workplace crèches, canteens, launderettes and other worker support services.

Women's waged work in rural areas has been highlighted by recent studies of the gender division of labour, notably in Zimbabwe (Adams 1991) and Tanzania (Mbilinyi 1989, 1991). In both contexts, the majority of women in waged work are agricultural workers, and women constitute a high proportion of the paid agricultural workforce, as well as performing a great deal of unpaid agricultural work. Both authors provide extensive quantitative data to illustrate women's high level of participation in paid agricultural work, with Mbilinyi arguing that the employment of such large numbers of women is part and parcel of the increased use of more easily exploited casual labour, which is hired seasonally and more cheaply than full time workers, most of whom are male. Mbilinyi (1989, 1991) argues that the hiring of casual and female labour has reduced the wage bill in public and private enterprises, with women consistently receiving lower wages than men for the same work requiring the same qualifications, a tradition which she traces back to the colonial plantation economy.

Adams (1991) presents a useful analysis of female wage labour in rural Zimbabwe, one which dispels a number of myths about rural African households. In particular, the preponderance of women among rural wage workers, particularly those involved in low-paid and casual work undermines the notion of women as being mainly involved in small-holder food production on family plots. The survey material she cites also demonstrates how important it is to distinguish between two types of female-headed household: female-male households on the one hand, which are headed by women while deriving much benefit from the remittances and property of an absentee husband, and women-only households run by single women, who are in the weakest economic position of all social groups. Many of the women-men households are relatively well-off, with women managing sizeable farms, hiring waged labour and owning cattle, ploughs and other factors of production. The fact that the data she has collected in Masvingo Province indicate that as many as 97 per cent receive some remittance from their absent spouses also challenges a notion prevalent in literature on the colonial period, namely that of female-headed households as households abandoned by men.

Women's employment as waged plantation workers has also been examined, notably by participants at a 1992 Centre for Basic Research (CBR) workshop, 'Women and Work'. Asowa-Okwe's contribution looks at tea and rice plantations in Uganda, noting the increased employment of women in all aspects of plantation work, alongside men in the fields as well as in conventionally 'feminine' roles of typists and canteen workers. Nonetheless, male workers still predominate and display negative attitudes towards women workers. Within the household, men do not share either the domestic or the food growing tasks, backbreaking duties that women continue to perform in addition to their waged work. While the penetration of capitalism has wrought changes in labour, including the increased involvement of women, it appears not to have affected the patriarchal relations that have prevailed within the household since pre-colonial and colonial times.

Mbilinyi (1992) carried out an action research project in collaboration with worker organisations to elucidate the situation of women workers on Tanzanian sugar cane plantations, where women have been employed since the early 1980s. Despite the generally favourable attitude of employers towards the efficiency and skill of women workers, gender discrimination and sexual harassment were both identified as problems which undermined wages and job security for all workers, by allowing for women to be paid lower wages than men, and to be hired as casual labour, both of which could be used to undermine the position of male waged workers. Like Asowa-Okwe (1992), Mbilinyi (1992) addresses the need for greater sharing in the domestic sphere, and/or greater provision of support in the form of childcare, canteens, recreation and public systems of fuel and water.

The Informal Sector

One could almost be forgiven for developing the impression that women dominate the African informal sector, so copious has been the literature on women's participation within it. The question of whether women actually do predominate in the informal sector is posed, but not answered directly by Friedman and Hambridge (1991). Instead they point out the 'hidden' nature of many of women's informal activities, and the fact that in some South African studies women appear to outnumber men. However, a great many African men too have no waged employment, because the formal sector has always been small in relation to the size of the adult working population of most African countries. This is why so many of the income earning activities that African men and women undertake fall into the category of informal work: most of them are unwaged, irregular, small scale activities that are unsupported and unregulated by any institutional or policy framework. The fact that men prevail in the formal sector does not mean that women enjoy any advantage in the informal sector. Here too there is a marked sexual division of labour, and the more lucrative and skilled kinds of informal work (roadside mechanics, profitable areas of trade, plumbing, building, electrical repair-shops, labouring, etc.) have remained the preserve of men. Correspondingly, one finds that women predominate only in those areas which are extensions of their existing domestic and reproductive roles, and often require little or no training. Typically, women engage in brewing, food production and selling, trading, craft production, piecework and services such as sex work, laundering, catering and hairdressing. All these activities are characterised by flexibility of hours and location, and can be carried out from a home base, and so are easily combined with motherhood and other domestic duties.

Conceptually, studies of women's informal activities show the reproductive and productive domains to be so intimately interlinked that they cannot really be separated, so making nonsense of the manner in which both policies and theories have relied on a division between the two. The situation is further complicated by the fact that many women engage in several different activities simultaneously, or change their activities over time. Studies of women's informal work also highlight the intricate and interdependent relationship between what is defined as formal and what is defined as informal activity, and the artificiality of treating these as separate spheres (see Horn 1994, below). A great many women engage in informal productive or trading activities alongside their formal employment. In agriculture it is even more obvious that growing crops for the market and growing crops for own-consumption are intimately bound up, and structured by complex and changing gender relations. The crops that a woman grows on her land might be for both subsistence and cash, with the family consuming some, and the surplus being sold on the domestic market as a cash crop, or processed and sold within a social network.

A further consideration to be borne in mind is the legality of the activities. Development researchers and policy-makers have tended to focus on the unproscribed activities that conform to dominant notions of entrepreneurialism, and which can be regarded as acceptable capitalist activities, of the kind which should be developed to mitigate the contraction of the formal sector. Yet a significant percentage of the more lucrative informal activities are carried on outside the realm of the law. This may involve the unlicensed production and sale of a commodity, for example beer, which although a legal product, is officially regulated and restricted. Or it may involve the production and/or distribution of illegal goods or services (drug-trafficking, illicit arms production, sex work). Smuggling may involve either legal or illegal goods, but is itself an underground activity. The social implications and risks of participating in less-than-legal or illegal activities vary accordingly, with some of the literature advocating the acceptance of those informal activities like brewing - which do not involve producing or handling illegal commodities (Meagher, personal communication).

In short, the methodological and practical problems that arise when one attempts to assess the extent to which women are involved in informal work are immense. Detailed time allocation studies are expensive and time consuming, but provide a valuable way to reveal the realities that labour force surveys and national statistics obfuscate.

Brewing and petty trading in urban areas are popular activities that have attracted research attention. Several recent studies focus on the entrepreneurial survival strategies deployed by women in their eternal struggle to mitigate the effects of deteriorating economic conditions, rather than on the concept of informal sector *per se*. Mbilinyi's (1992) Tanzanian study illustrates women are not just engaging in supplementary activity (as in supplementing a male wage), with a growing number of women contributing significantly towards family incomes, if not becoming the main breadwinners in their households. That this has long been the case in parts of West Africa deserves more attention, particularly when research aims to considering the motivations and conditions under which women engage in various forms of work.

Horn (1994) suggests in her book *Cultivating Customers*, that in Zimbabwe, urban women have long engaged in the petty trading of fresh market produce. She theorises that urban women deprived of the garden plots they traditionally farm to provision their families, fulfill their gender roles by working hard at fresh produce vending. This enables them to earn an independent and unmonitored income in a manner compatible with looking after young children, as well as to provide food for their families through their wholesale purchasing, and consumption of unsold perishables. Horn's anthropological background surfaces when she probes the psychological and cultural motivations, positing that Harare market women value their customers in the same way that their rural equivalents value their harvests, viewing abundance as a sign of having won the favour of their husband's ancestors (hence the title). They are thus motivated along traditional gender lines, but in a way that allows them to carve out a niche for themselves in an otherwise insecure and potentially alienating urban setting. Detailed fieldwork is presented in an intelligible style, and Horn is so impressed with the high level of initiative and entrepreneurialism she discovers in Harare's market women that she cannot understand how the World Bank and IMF have been so slow to recognise the 'model' of independent, individualised labour that they provide. She regards the marginalisation of women's informal activities as a result, not just of gender inequality, but also as an artefact of the false division of the economy into formal and informal sectors. Her findings lead her to call on policy makers to do away with this dualistic division, and instead to regard the economy as a unified whole, within which women's micro-enterprises can be accorded due regard.

In the rural areas too, women's informal activities have gained importance in the context of falling real wage levels, and this is reflected in the growing research attention to the rural informal sector, much of it exploring the possibility of rural entrepreneurialism offering a cure for growing rural poverty. Here the virtual absence of the option of formal employment for either sex, and even less for women than for men, has meant that the vast majority of rural Africans continue to labour on the land, both formally and informally. Most rural women farm small plots or vegetable gardens, and rear poultry and other small animals. In some locations, women are involved in pottery, weaving, bead-making, knitting and other types of craft production, as well as the inevitable petty trading of such products.

Many such activities have been targeted by Women In Development (WID) projects and credit schemes, presuming that herein lies a panacea for the impoverishment of rural women, and the poor health and nutrition of rural children. The research indicates that these tend to be subsistence rather than wealth-producing activities, and this is not easy to change. Most rural women's informal activities are prevented from being more lucrative by the problems of transportation, lack of markets, lack of capital and limited access to equipment, tools and the labour of others (Preston-Whyte and Nene 1991, Preston-Whyte 1991, Mackintosh 1989). These and other writings on the subject caution against investing hope that the rural informal sector can solve the problems of rural underdevelopment, in the way that many of the architects of market reforms wish, because it is wealth and demand which create opportunity, and both are lacking in most rural areas.

Kyomuhendo's (1992) study of women's involvement in the rural informal sector in Uganda reiterates the general depiction and conclusions reached by the (mostly South African) work discussed above, noting the importance of petty commodity production and commerce in the rural Ugandan economy, and that women's participation in it has increased as a result of the adverse economic realities in the country. Here the situation is one of multiple disadvantage, and in this context even the most innovative and industrious efforts of women do not guarantee their survival.

The rural informal sector is the subject of growing attention at conferences and in unpublished reports, and likely to continue to be so for some time to come, given the persistence of rural impoverishment in most of the region, and the particularly disadvantaged situation of rural women.

Sex Work

Sex work has received much attention from the authorities, and been rendered illicit to varying degrees by successive colonial and post-colonial administrations. As a significant informal sector activity, it has seldom been considered in recent studies adopting the fashionable focus on entrepreneurialism, presumably because of its illegality and stigmatization. While few African regimes (if any) have advocated legalization of the sex trade, and many have invoked it as a social scourge in campaigns of harassment and forced removal of women from the urban areas, it has more often been tacitly accepted. However, because sex workers are left to operate outside the law, they are also unable to exercise even the most basic human rights, remaining vulnerable to abuses perpetrated by the authorities as well as their clients.

Current publications on African prostitution are worth examining in some detail here because, like female genital mutilation, it has been a site of both activism and research in women's studies internationally, with a number of studies addressing its various manifestations in Africa. African research is the same as that carried out elsewhere in that it focuses on the women, rather than on the organisation of the trade. Male management of female prostitution, the customers that sustain the trade, and the connections between the sex trade, militarisation and international tourism have all received far less attention than the activities of women engaged in providing sexual services. Male prostitution, while visible particularly at tourist sites, is also largely ignored, even in the AIDs literature.

Recent African studies looking at female prostitution have contributed to a deeper understanding of broader property and exchange relations between the sexes, historically, and in the context of rapid social and economic transformations (e.g. White 1990, Dirasse 1991, Naanen 1991), even where the research has been motivated by health concerns (e.g. Pickering et al. 1992, Pickering and Wilkins 1993).

The small but significant body of knowledge on the whys and wherefores of sex work in Africa has taken us a long way beyond Cutrufelli's (1983:33) ridiculous remark that 'either overtly or covertly, prostitution is still the main if not the only source of work for African women'. If early work seemed to support the view that African women were hapless victims of circumstance, forced into prostitution to feed their children because of their oppression and marginalisation, recent studies emphasize the different options (albeit within the informal sector) available to women, and suggest that sex work presents an attractive choice because of its relative lucrativeness, and the fact that it is not characterised by the long hours of unrelenting drudgery demanded by other forms of work available to women.

Dirasse's (1991) study of prostitution in Addis Ababa furnishes us with the first major study of women's involvement in sex work in contemporary Africa. Following White's (1991) study of the sex trade and property accumulation in colonial Nairobi, Dirasse too lays out detailed information on the various types of sexual and marital relationships, and the forms and levels of prostitution. She begins by noting that Addis Ababa is distinguished among African cities by having a preponderance of women, even among the young migrant population that is usually assumed to be male. This observation raises a question: given that prostitution is commonly viewed as being a concomitant to the presence of single male migrants in African towns, how has it become so popular an activity when women outnumber men? The fact that as many as 25 per cent (1975 figures) of Addis Ababa's female population are prostitutes cannot be fully explained by the 'lonely men' thesis, but requires further explanation. Dirasse begins by contextualising what is meant by prostitution, delineating seven main relational patterns prevalent in urban Ethiopia.

The most devout members of the Coptic Church practice *kurban*, a strict religious marriage that is not only for life, but demands celibacy of the survivor after the death of either partner. *Semanya* (civil marriage) is also regarded as permanent, as is *nika* (polygamous marriage which is both jural and Islamic).

These three are all co-residential and oblige the woman to provide both domestic and sexual services in exchange for security, respectability, status, a home and other such blessings. A less permanent but nonetheless contractual arrangement known as demoz is widely practised among less privileged classes and involves payment for domestic and sexual services over a time that may range from a week to several years. Mistresses (komot) are in less formally contracted relationships, in which the woman is loyal to a visiting man who bestows gifts and/or money in return for her sexual favours (rather like the traditional karuwanci in Hausaland).

In the case of *woshoma*, the parties are lovers, no payments are required from either side, nor is there any formal contract. The relational form that Dirasse identifies as most closely approximating the English prostitution is known in Amharic as *setana adarii*. This is the only form which allows the woman to have more than one partner, by hiring her services informally without religious or jural sanction, on a temporary basis, and receiving payment for sexual services. Such women are not stigmatized by members of their own class, and indeed, if successful, may be quite well-respected figures in their communities. It is this group that are regarded as prostitutes for the purposes of the study.

Within this group she identifies a further six sub-groups ranging from the lowest level streetwalkers to the top level madames, who own large bars or clubs which employ young women to work as bar consorts. Upward mobility within the trade is hindered by the competition rather than by the class or caste origins of the practitioners. She finds that sex workers come from a wide range of social and economic backgrounds, but whether they are rural migrants or school drop-outs they tend to have above average education levels. Dirasse's analysis suggests that for Ethiopian women prostitution is a strategic occupational choice, rather than a last resort. Nonetheless, its incidence in related to the inaccessibility of the formal labour market to women.

Historically, she locates the prevalence of the practice in the dominance of Addis Ababa by Amhara culture, in which various alternatives to marriage are widely accepted, a tolerance that derives from earlier systems of courtesanship and domestic slavery. However, the advent of modern, commoditised prostitution bereft of relational subtleties or courtship niceties is linked with the arrival of Italians and the forced recruitment of thousands of young women to service the Italian soldiers during the 1930s. Today rural-urban disparities in development, the continuing limited access of women to education, property ownership and the labour market, and the presence of large numbers of men unable to afford more permanent relationships, are all identified as making prostitution a viable option for women in Addis Ababa. Because she centres her analysis on local economic conditions, Dirasse does not explore the possible effects of the sizeable and affluent international community in Addis Ababa on the lives and choices of these women, or whether outward migration offers an alternative, or improves prospects. Overall it is a study unique in its depth and debunks a great many of the prevailing misconceptions about the commoditisation of African sexual relations.

The Gambian research (Pickering et al. 1992, Pickering & Wilkins 1993) shows prostitutes to be a highly mobile group, in this case mainly within Gambia and between Senegal and Gambia. Here too women identified as prostitutes have above average levels of education and enjoy a somewhat higher-than-average standard of living. Most (all but 9 per cent) of the 248 prostitutes in the study had non-Gambian ethnic origins, and half of their clients were not Gambians themselves.

The research reported deliberately excludes the prostitution associated with the tourist industry from consideration, so that here too, international relations are not considered beyond noting that coastal tourist hotels have generated a class of more highly paid sex workers. These studies, funded by the Gambian Medical Research Council are both primarily concerned with the spread of HIV/AIDS. As such they concentrate on the behaviour of prostitutes, particularly their mobility and use of condoms, rather than on any broader socio-economic or cultural analysis. Nonetheless, their findings concur with Dirasse's view that women are not so much driven to prostitution by destitution or having hungry families to feed, as attracted into a relatively lucrative trade that they can combine with other economic activities, and engage in on a part-time basis to more than adequately satisfy their material needs.

Conclusion: Whither African Women's Studies?

What conclusions can be drawn from so diverse a body of material on such challenging subject matter? In the course of this review, much of the material has necessarily been treated summarily, with a view to indicating the current state of the art. In so doing I have outlined main research directions and themes, and pointed out obvious gaps in the research. My aim has been to make an overview of the field available to African scholars, rather than to conduct the kind of detailed analysis that would precede specific research projects or programmes. A review of this nature should also be of use to teachers in the growing numbers of courses now running in African universities, for whom access to new material frequently poses difficulties. In addition to reviewing the material, I have also paid some attention to the methodological innovations favoured by scholars in this area.

In the introduction I indicated the need for more indigenous scholarship, and greater support for indigenous scholars. The material reviewed here demonstrates that there is still a predominance of Western-based scholarship, albeit of increasingly high quality. The obvious prejudices and preconceptions of earlier work have benefited from the critiques of African scholars, but Bozzoli's 'Bantu sociologists' are still not getting published as much as they should be, and few African scholars are attaining international recognition as theorists in their fields of interest.

The key role that African academic and research institutions must play in the struggle for the Africanization of women's studies in Africa cannot be overstated. It is through these that funding and publication of African scholars will be made possible, on African terms. The drain of quality scholars into WID consultancy work, rather than into independent intellectual production affects gender research and women's studies as profoundly as it does other areas. The financing and institutional support of African scholarship has already been identified as a major constraint on academic freedom (see Diouf and Mamdani 1994), and one which leads many intellectuals to 'self-censor' their work (Imam and Mama 1994).

Self-censorship leads many of us to avoid possibly controversial areas of research, or to concentrate efforts solely on those subjects most likely to receive the sponsorship of funding agencies. In this way, gender and women's studies are either avoided, or only 'safe' areas are addressed, in an opportunistic manner that does a disservice both to the goals of the international women's movement that has given birth to the whole field, and to the African women who are the objects of study.

A number of national and regional research institutions already express their commitment to supporting gender research and women's studies in the region, and have taken preliminary steps in the right direction. While some of this commitment is beginning to filter through in journals (notably Africa Development, East African Social Science Review, and the recently launched Southern African Feminist Review) and magazines (*SAPEM monthly* and Echo), we are still awaiting more in the way of books and monographs.

More independent research sponsorship and publication in gender and women's studies is not however the only measure required to redress the situation. It is also necessary for existing research sponsoring institutions to conduct outreach work to identify potential scholars who can be commissioned to undertake and coordinate research efforts, and to produce the publications. The most often-heard complaint of those taking or teaching courses on gender and women's studies is the paucity and unavailability of African material, as my own experience teaching African postgraduate students of women's studies indicates. Very often it is students and teachers who may be sufficiently motivated to change the situation. Existing programmes, their staff and their students thus provide the most obvious human resource to be tapped in furthering the development of African women's studies and gender research.

The last few years have seen a great proliferation of national networks (like the Tanzanian Gender Networking programme, the Network for Women's Studies in Nigeria), programmes, units and centres committed to the furtherance of women's studies across the African region (see ASA 1991, Musoke 1992, Mama 1996). The majority of these suffer from the same financial and infrastructural weaknesses hindering all academic production, and continue to rely on a high level of voluntarism from committed women scholars. However, the gatherings that have brought African women scholars together to consider the agenda of gender and women's studies in the region, and to explore strategies for enhancing the institutional bases from which teaching and research in women' studies can best be carried out all indicate an unprecedented level of enthusiasm, a desire for independent scholarship and an awareness of the different opportunities that lie within this broad and changing rubric.

Regional and national diversities notwithstanding, there is less discussion and less clarity on the politics of women's studies in the region. The only consensual point is that most of us would prefer there to be more African women scholars involved in the theoretical and empirical production of women's studies. There is far less consensus concerning the issue of whether or not academic studies of women are, or should be, linked to a broadly defined women's movement, or directed towards facilitating gender equality. There is not even much consensus on using the term 'women's studies' which is often jettisoned in favour of 'gender' to gain acceptability among the men and allow them to feel, and be, included. 'Feminism' as a term and a concept, is now marginally less contentious than it was a few years ago. Although there are not yet many 'centres for feminist studies' in Africa, there is an increasing acceptance of the goal of 'gender equality' if not 'women's liberation'. The first of these, the Centre for Feminist Studies in Harare is currently being established. African feminists, who define themselves as such are becoming more vocal and outspoken, but remain, as elsewhere a minority voice both within the academies and in the world of policy, power and decision-making. This too is reflected in indigenous studies of women.

As the field continues to grow within the region, it will become more possible to discern the still-embryonic national and regional characteristics within African women's studies, trends that are increasingly in evidence even now, when one considers the preoccupations of say, North African women scholars as compared to South Africans, or Kenyans as compared to Nigerians. There is enormous scope for regular workshops, conferences and publications to facilitate the much-needed exchanges between the growing pool of local scholars, within particular countries, within sub-regions, and across the region, on particular themes. The list of themes which have never been addressed at any regional forum is a long and open-ended one, which we could do well to shorten.

Bibliography

AAWORD. 1992, 'Women and Reproduction in Africa', Occasional Paper Series No. 5, Dakar, AAWORD.

AAWORD, 1992, 'Women and the Mass Media in Africa', Occasional Paper Series No 6, Dakar, AAWORD.

AAWORD, undated, 'Women as Agents and Beneficiaries of Development Assistance', Occasional Paper Series no.4, Dakar, AAWORD.

Abdalla, R., 1982, *Sisters in Affliction: Circumcision and Infibulation of Women in Africa*, London, Zed.

Abdullah, H., 1993, 'Transition Politics and the Challenge of Gender in Nigeria', *Review of African Political Economy*, N 56, pp. 27-41, Oxford.

Adams, J., 1991, 'Female Wage Labour in Rural Zimbabwe', *World Development* 19 (2/3), pp. 163-177.

Adepoju, A., Oppong, C., 1994, eds., *Gender, Work and Population in Sub-Saharan Africa*, London, James Currey.

Adesina, J., 1992, *Labour Movements and Policy-making in Africa*, Working Paper, Dakar, CODESRIA.

Afonja, S., Aina, B., 1995, eds., *Nigerian Women in Social Change*, Programme in Women's Studies, Ile-Ife, Obafemi Awolowo University.

African Studies Association (ASA), 1991, 'The Status of Women's Studies in Africa', unpublished papers presented at Women's Caucus Workshop, St Louis Missouri, U.S.A. 23-16 November.

Ahikire, J., 1992, 'Gender and Labour Processes: An Analysis of Gender Dynamics in United Garment Industry Limited (UGIL)', CBR Uganda,Workshop Paper.

Ahlberg, B.M., 1990, 'African Culture and Development: Changing Sexuality in Sub-Saharan Africa and its Impact on Women's Reproductive Health', Annual Meeting of Swedish Sociological Association, Gavle, Feb. 1-3 1990.

Ahonsi, Babatunde A., 1995, 'Gender Relations, Demographic Change and the Prospects for Sustainable Development in Africa', *Africa Development*, Vol. XX, n 4, pp. 58-114, Dakar, CODESRIA.

Akuffo, A., 1990, 'Dimensions of Sex Discrimmination: The Ghanaian Working Women's Experience', Greenhill Journal of Administration, Vol. 7, N 3, 4, pp. 76-107.

Allman, J., 1991, "Of 'Spinsters', 'Concubines' and 'Wicked Women': Reflections on Gender and Social Change in Colonial Asante", *Gender and History*, Vol. 3, N 2, pp. 176-189.

Altorki S. and El Sohl C.F.eds., 1988, *Arab Women in the Field: Studying Your Own Society*, Syracuse, Syracuse University Press.

Amadiume, I., 1987, *Male Daughters, Female Husbands*, London, Zed Books.

Amali, E., 1989, 'The Role of Women in Agricultural Development Process' *Development Studies Review*, Vol. 3, N 1-2, pp. 52-61, Univ. of Jos.

American Sociological Association, 1991, Papers from presented at the Panel on 'Women's Studies in Africa', St Louis, Missouri, U.S.A. Nov. 22-23.

Amos, V., Parmar, P., 1984 'Challenging Imperial Feminism', *Feminist Review* 17.

Anyanwu, J.C., 1991, 'Women, Education and the Use of Bank Credit in Nigeria: Challenges for the twenty-first Century' *UFAHAMU*, Vol. XIX, N 2-3, pp. 130-145.

Arabsheibani, G., 1990, 'Higher Education and the Occupational Status of Women in Egypt', *Journal of Asian and African Studies*, Vol. XV, N 3-4, pp. 213-218.

Ardayfio-Schandorf, E., 1990, 'Ghanaian Women in the Formal Sector: Social Mobility Through Education' *Greenhill Journal of Administration*, Vol. 7, N 3-4, pp. 153-171.

Arhin, K., 1983, 'The Political and Military Roles of Akan Women' in C. Oppong' ed., *Female and Male in West Africa*, London, George Allen and Unwin.

Arhin, K.; 1992, *The Life and Work of Kwame Nkrumah*, Accra, Sedco.

Asowa-Okwe, C., 1992, 'Women Wage Workers in Plantation Estates in Uganda', Kampala CBR, Workshop Paper.
Atieno, R., Hayanagh, R., 1992, 'Women's Role in Agricultural Food Production in Kenya: The Case of Siaya District', *Eastern Africa Social Science Review*, Vol. 8, N 2, pp. 36-50.
Awe, B., 1992, ed., *Nigerian Women in Historical Perspective Sankore*, Lagos/Ibadan, Bookcraft.
Ayoade, J. A. A., Nwabuzor, E. J., Sambo, W. A. eds., 1992, *Women and Politics in Nigeria*, Abuja Centre for Democratic Studies.
Babangida, M., 1988, *The Home Front: Nigerian Army Officers and their Wives*, Ibadan, Fountain Publications.
Badran, M., 1991a, 'Competing Agendas: Feminists, Islam and the State in 19th and 20th Century Egypt' in Kandioyoti (1991).
Badran, M., 1991b, 'Gender Activism: Feminists and Islamists in Egypt' in Moghadam (1991).
Badran, M., 1994, 'Dual Liberation: Feminism and Nationalism in Egypt', 1970-1925, *Feminist Issues*, Vol. 8, N 1.
Badri, A., E., 1991, 'Women in Management and Administration in Sudan' *Ahfad Journal*, Vol. 8, N 2, pp. 5-24.
Baffoun, A., 1994, 'Feminism and Muslim Fundamentalism: The Tunisian and Algerian Cases' *Africa Development*, Vol. 19, N 2, pp. 5-20.
Barnes, T. A., 1992, 'The Fight for Control of African Women's Mobility in Colonial Zimbabwe, 1900-1939' *Signs*, Vol. 17, N 3, pp. 586-608.
Beale, J., 1990, 'Women under Indentured Labour in Colonial Natal, 1860-1911' in Walker (1982).
Bello, M., 1991, 'Women Organising Under Structural Adjustment Programme', Workshop Paper on Women Organising in the Process of Industrialisation, The Netherlands, ISS.
Beneria, L., 1981, 'Conceptualising the Labour Force: The Underestimation of Women's Economic Activities' in Nelson (1981).
Beneria, L., and Sen, G., 1981, 'Accumulation, Reproduction and Women's Role in Economic Development: Boserup Revisited' in *Signs*, Vol. 7, N 2.
Berger, I., 1992, *Threads of Solidarity*, Bloomington, Indiana University Press, London, James Currey.
Bola, Udegbe I., 1995, 'Better Life for Rural Women Programme: An Agenda for Positive Change?' *Africa Development*, Vol. XX, n 4, pp. 69-84, Dakar CODESRIA.
Bonner, P., 1990, 'Desirable or Undesirable Basotho Women?' Liquor, Prostitution and the Migration of Basotho Women to the Rand, 1920-1945' in Walker 1990.
Boutta, C., Cherifati-Merabtine, D., 1994, 'The Social Representation of Women in Algeria's Islamist Movement' in Moghadam 1994 a.
Bozzoli, B., 1991, *Women of Phokeng: Consciousness, Life Strategy and Migrancy in South Africa*, 1990-1983, Portsmouth/London, Heineman/James Currey.
Buchert, L., 1993, 'A Gender Perspective on Adult Literacy: Some Lessons from Dodoma Region', *AALAE Journal*, Vol. 7, N 1, pp. 7-23.
Bujra, J., 1990, 'Taxing Development: Why Must Women Pay? Gender and the Development Debate in Tanzania', Review of African Political Economy *ROAPE* 47.
Byanyima, W. Karagwa, 1992, 'Women in Political Struggle in Uganda' in Bystydzienski (1992).
Bystydzienski, J. M., 1992, Women Transforming Politics: worldwide strategies for empowerment, Bloomington, Indiana University Press.
Callaway, H., 1987, *Gender, Culture and Empire: European Women in Colonial Nigeria*, London, St. Anthony's/Macmillan.
Callway, B. and Creevey, L., 1994, *The Heritage of Islam: Women, Religion and Politics in West Africa*, Boulder and London, Lynne Rienner.
Campbell, H., 1993, 'Angolan Women and the Electoral Process in Angola, 1992' *Africa Development*, Vol. 18, N 2, pp. 23-63.
Carby, H., 1982, 'White Women Listen! Black Feminism and the Boundaries of Sisterhood' in *The Empire Strikes Back: Race and Racism in 70s Britain, Hutchinson*, London, Centre for Contemporary Cultural Studies, Birmingham University.

Carney, J. and Watts, M., 1990, 'Manufacturing Dissent: Work, Gender and the Politics of Meaning in a Peasant Society' *Africa*, Vol. 60, N 2, pp. 207-241.

Carney, J., 1991, 'Disciplining Women? Rice, Mechanization, and the Evolution of Mandinka Gender Relations in Senegambia' *Signs*, Vol. 16, N 4, pp. 651-681.

Casimiro, I, Liberman, G, and Osorio, C., 1991, 'The Status of Women's Studies in Africa: Research on Women and Gender in Mozambique' ASA Conference paper.

Centre for Basic Research (CBR), 1992, 'Women and Work : Historical Trends' CBR Workshop, Sept 7-10 1992, Kampala.

Chazan, N., 1989, 'Gender Perspectives on African States' in Parpart and Staudt 1989.

Cheater, A., 1990, 'The Ideology of Communal Land Tenure in Zimbabwe: Mythogenesis Enacted?' *Africa*, Vol. 60, N 2, pp. 188-206.

Cheriet, B., 1992, Islamism and Feminism: Algeria's "Rites of Passage" to Democracy in J. P., Entelis and PC., Naylor (1992).

Cobham, R., 1992, 'Misgendering the Nation: African Nationalist Fictions and *Muruddin Farah's Maps*', in Parker A. *et al.* (ed.) Nationalisms and Sexualities, London and New York, Routledge.

Cock, J., 1989, *Maids and Madams: Domestic Workers Under Apartheid*, London, The Women's Press.

Cock, J., 1990, 'Domestic Service and Education for Domesticity: The Incorporation of Xhosa Women into Colonial Society' in Walker 1989.

Cock, J., 1992, *Women and War in South Africa*, London, Open Letters.

CODESRIA, 1994, *Bibliography on Gender*, Dakar, CODESRIA.

Creevey, L., 1991, 'The Impact of Islam on Women in Senegal', *Journal Developing Areas*, Vol. 25, pp. 347-368.

Crumbley, D. H., 1992, 'Impurity and Power: Women in Aladura Churches', *Africa*, Vol. 62, N 4, pp. 505-521.

Currie, D. and Kazi, H., 1987, 'Academic Feminism and the Process of Deradicalization: Re-examining the Issues' *Feminist Review*, Vol. 25, pp. 77-98.

Cutrufelli, M.R., 1983, *Women of Africa: Roots of Oppression*, London, Zed.

Davis, S. S., 1992, 'Impediments to Empowerment: Moroccan Women and the Agencies' in *Journal of Developing Societies*, Vol. 8, No 1, pp. 111-121.

Davison, J., 1992, 'Changing Relations of Production in Southern Malawi's Households: Implications for Involving Rural Women in Development' in *Journal of Contemporary African Studies*, Vol. 2, No 1, pp. 72-84.

De Beauvoir, S., 1972, *The Second Sex*, Harmondsworth, Penguin. [First edition 1949].

Denzer, L., 1989, *Women in Government Service in Colonial Nigeria, 1862-1945*, Boston University African Studies Centre, Working Paper 136.

Denzer, L., 1992, 'Domestic Science Training in Colonial Yorubaland' in Hansen (1992).

Dijkman, H. and VanDijk, M.P., 1993, 'Female Entrepreneurs in the Informal Sector of Ouagadougou' *Development Policy Review*, Vol. 2, pp. 273-288.

Diop, C.A., 1974, *The African Origin of Civilization: Myth or Reality*, Westport, Lawrence Hill and Co.

Diop, C.A., 1987, *Precolonial Black Africa*, Westport, Lawrence Hill and Co.

Diouf, M. and Mamdani, M. eds., 1994, *Academic Freedom in Africa*, Dakar, CODESRIA.

Dirasse, L., 1991, *The Commoditization of Female Sexuality: Prostitution and Socio-economic Relations in Addis Ababa*, Ethiopia, New York, AMS.

Dolphyne, F.A., 1991, *The Emancipation of Women: An African Perspective*, Accra, Ghana Univ. Press.

Due, J.M. and White-Jones, M., 1989, 'Difference in Earning, Labour Inputs, Decision-making and Perception of Development Between Farm and Market: A Case Study in Zambia' *Eastern African Economic Review* 5, Vol. 2, pp. 92-103.

Early, E., 1993, *Baladi Women of Cairo: Playing with an Egg and a Stone*, Boulder & London Lynne Rienner.

El Amouri Institute, 1993, 'Women's Role in the Informal Sector in Tunisia' in Massiah.

El Dareer, A., 1982, *Women, Why do you Weep? Circumcision and its consequences*, London, Zed.

El Nagar, S., 1991, 'The Status of Women's Studies in the Sudan', ASA Conference Paper, 22-23 Nov., St Louis, U.S.A.

El Sadaawi, N., 1980, *The Hidden Face of Eve: Women of the Arab World*, London, The Women's Press.

El Samani, M.O., 1990, 'The Structure of Agricultural Production and the Role of Women in Different Farming Systems in Western Sudan with an Emphasis on Traditional Agriculture' *Ahfad Journal* Vol. 7, No 2, pp. 4-26.

El-Bakri, Z. and Besha, R.M., 1989, 'Women in Development in Eastern Africa: An Agenda for Research', Proceedings of the OSSREA Workshop on Women and Development in Eastern Africa, Ethiopia, Nazareth.

El-Bakri, Z.B. and Khier, A.H., 1989, 'Sudanese Women in History and Historiography: A Proposed Strategy for Curriculum Change' NRC/SFPA Workshop on Women's Studies in Sudan.

El-Bakri, Z.B., 1989, 'Teaching Women' Studies at the Dept. of Sociology/Anthropology, University of Khartoum NCR/SFPA Women's Studies in the Sudan Workshop paper.

Elson, D., 1991, 'Male Bias in Macroeconomics: The Case of Structural Adjustment', in Elson 1991.

Enloe, C., 1989, *Bananas, Beaches and Bases: Making Feminist Sense of International Politics* London, Pandora.

Entelis, J.P. and Naylor P.C., 1992 eds., *State and Society in Algeria*, Boulder, Westview.

Erinosho, L. and Bello-Imam, I. B., 1991, *Perspectives on Small-Scale Food Processing and Distribution Industries in Nigeria* Social Science Council of Nigeria/Ibadan, Vantage Publishers.

Eshete, A., 1991, 'The Status of Research on Women in Ethiopia' ASA Conference Paper.

Etta, Florence Ebam, 1994, 'Gender Issues in Contemporary African Education', *Africa Development*, Vol. XIX, n 4, pp. 57-84, Dakar, CODESRIA.

Fatton, R. 1989, 'Gender, Class, and State in Africa' in Parpart and Stuadt (1989).

Federation of Muslim Women's Associations in Nigeria, 1991, 'The Muslim Woman: Magazine of FOMWAN', Vol. 1, No 3, Minna.

Feldman-Savelsberg, P., 1994, 'Plundered Kitchens and Empty Wombs: Fear of Infertility in the Cameroonian Grasslands', *Social Science and Medicine* Vol. 39 No 4 pp. 463-474.

Frates, L. L., 1993, 'Women in the South African National Liberation Movement, 1948-1960: An Historiographical Overview', *UFAHAMU*, Vol. 21 No 1-2 pp. 27-39.

Friedman, M. and Hambridge, M., 1991, 'The Informal Sector, Gender and Development in E. Preston-Whyte and C Rogerson eds. *South Africa's Informal Economy*, Cape-Town, Oxford Univ.

Gaidzanwa, R., 1991, 'The Ideology of Domesticity and the Struggles of Women Workers Within and Outside Political Parties: The Case of Zimbabwe', Workshop Paper Women Organising in the Process of Industrialisation, The Hague, Institute of Social Studies.

Gaidzanwa, R., 1991, 'Women's Studies and Research on Women in Southern Africa: The Zimbabwe Case', ASA Conference Paper, St Louis, USA.

Gaidzanwa, R., 1993, 'Citizenship, Nationality, Gender and Class in Southern Africa' *Alternatives* Vol. 18 pp. 39-59.

Gaitskell, D. and Unterhalter, E., 1989, 'Mothers of the Nation: A Comparative Analysis of Nation, Race and Motherhood in Afrikaner Nationalism and the African National Congress' *in* Yuval-Davis and F. Anthias eds.

Grier, B., 1992, 'Pawns, Porters and Petty Traders: Women in the Transition to Cash Crop Agriculture in Colonial Ghana' *Signs* Vol. 17 No 2 pp. 304-328

Grunebaum, E., 1991, 'The Islamic Movement, Development and Health Education: Recent Changes in the Health of Rural Women in Central *Sudan Social Science and Medicine*, Vol. 33 No 6 pp. 637-645.

Gugler, J., 1989, 'Women Stay on the Farm no More: Changing Patterns of Rural-urban Migration in Sub-Saharan Africa' Office of Women in International Development, *WID Forum* 12, Michigan State University.

Guy, J., 1990, 'Gender Oppression in Southern Africa's Precapitalist Societies' in Walker (1990).

Hafkin N.J. and Bay E.G. eds., 1975, Women in Africa: Studies in Social and Economic Change, Stanford University Press, Stanford, California.

Hakiki-Talahite, F., 1992, 'Women, Economic Reforms and Politics', in L. Rudebeck ed. (1976).

Hale, S. 1994 'Gender, Religious Identity and Political mobilization in Sudan' in Moghadam, (1994b).

Hale, S., 1992, 'The Rise of Islam and the National Islamic Front in Sudan' *Review of African Political Economy*, Vol. 54, pp. 27-41.

Hansen, K. T., 1992a, 'Gender and Housing: The Case of Domestic Service in Lusaka', Africa, Vol. 62, No 2, pp. 248-265.

Hansen, K.T., 1992b ed., *African Encounters with Domesticity*, New Brunswick, Rutgers University Press.

Harris, B., 1993, *The Political Economy of the Southern African Periphery: Cottage Industries, Factories and Female Wage Labour in Swaziland Compared*, London, St Martin's Press.

Hassim, S., 1990, 'Equality Versus Authority: Inkatha and the Politics of Gender in Natal', *Politikon*, Vol. 17, No 2, pp. 99-114.

Hassim, S., 1991, 'Gender, Social Location and Feministic Politics in South Africa', *Transformations* No 15, pp. 65-81.

Hassim, S., 1993, 'Family, Motherhood and Zulu Nationalism: The Politics of the Inkatha Women's Brigade', *Feminist Review*, Vol. 43, pp. 1-25.

Helie-Lucas, M., 1987, 'Against Nationalism: The Betrayal of Algerian Women', *Trouble and Strife* 11.

Herbert, E., 1993, *Iron, Gender and Power: Rituals of Transformation in African Societies*, Bloomington, Indiana Univ. Press.

Hicks, E., 1993, *Infibulation: Female Mutilation in Islamic Northeastern Africa*, New Brunswick Transaction.

Hollos, M., 1991, 'Migration, Education, and the Status of Women in Southern Nigeria' *American Anthropologist*, Vol. 93, No 4, pp. 852-870.

Horn, N. E., 1994, *Cultivating Customers: Market Women in Harare, Zimbabwe*, London and Boulder, Lynne Rienner.

Horn, P., 1991, 'Post-Apartheid South Africa: What About Women's Emancipation? *Transformation*, No 15, pp. 25-88.

Horn, P., 1992, Women and Work in South Africa: Transforming the World of Women's Work Through Initiative and Struggle', CBR Workshop Paper.

Hountoundji, P., 1983, *African Philosophy: Myth and Reality*, London, Hutchinson.

Hunt, D.L.S., 1993, 'The Changing Role of Women in African Music', *UFAHAMU*, Vol. XXI, No 1-2, pp. 41-49.

Hunt, N.R., 1990, 'Domesticity and Colonialism in Belgian Africa: Usumbura's Foyer Social, 1946-1960' in *Signs*, Vol. 15, No 3.

Hunt, N.R., 1992, 'Colonial Fairy Tales and the Knife and Fork Doctrine in the Heart of Africa' in Hansen 1992 Ed.

Ibeanu, O., 1992, 'Women and Elections in Nigeria: Some Empirical Evidence from the December 1991 Elections in Enugu State' *UFAHAMU*, Vol. 20, No 3, pp. 64-85.

Ibie, N.O., 1992, 'Media/Cultural Imperialism and Nigerian Women: Whose Culture, Which Imperialism?' *Journal of Social Development in Africa*, Vol. 7, No 2, pp. 39-52.

Imam, A., Mama, A. and Sow, F. eds. (forthcoming), *Engendering African Social Science*, Dakar CODESRIA.

Imam, A. and Mama, A., 1994, 'The Role of Academics in Constraining Academic Freedom', in Mamdani and Diouf (1994).

Imam, A., 1988, 'Gender Analysis and African Social Sciences in the 1990s' Paper to CODESRIA Roundtable of African Social Science in the 1990s, Dakar.

Imam, A., 1994, 'Politics, Islam, and Women in Kano', Northern Nigeria in Moghadam (1994a).

Inhorn, M. C., 1994, 'Kabsa (a.k.a Mushahara) and threatened fertility in Egypt', *Social Science and Medicine*, Vol. 39, No 4, pp. 487-505.

Ityavyar, D. A. and Obiajunwa, S. N., 1992, *The State and Women in Nigeria*, Jos, Univ. of Jos.

Jacobs, S., 1989, 'Zimbabwe: State, Class, and Gendered Models of Land Resettlement' in Parpart and Staudt (1989).
Jaggar and Bordo, 1989, *Gender/Body/Knowledge - Feminist Reconstructions of Being and Knowing*, New Brunswick, Rutgers University Press.
Kabira W., Oduol J. and Nzomo M., 1993, *Democratic Change in Africa: Women's Perspective*, Nairobi, AAWORD/ACTS.
Kabira, W. M. and Nzioki, E. A., 1993, *Celebrating Women's Resistance: A Case Study of the Women's Groups Movement in Kenya*.
Kandioyoti, D. eds., 1991, *Women, Islam and the State*, London, Macmillan.
Kanjir, N. and Jazdowska, N., 1993, 'Structural Adjustment and Women in Zimbabwe', *Review of African Political Economy*, No 56, pp. 11-26.
Kapteijns, L., 1994, 'Women and the Crisis of Communal Identity: The Cultural Construction of Gender in Somali History' in Samater 1984 ed.
Katz, C.A., 1990, 'Sexual Solidarity and the Secrets of Sight and Sound: Shifting Gender Relations and Their Ceremonial Constitution', *American Ethnologist*, Vol. 17, No 3, pp. 449-469.
Kenyon, S.M., 1991, *Five Women of Sennar: Culture and Change in Central Sudan*, Oxford, Clarendon.
Khasiani, S.A., and Njiro, E.I., 1993, *The Women's Movement in Kenya*, AAWORD, Nairobi.
Khennas, S. eds., 1993, *Industrialisation, Mineral Resources and Energy in Africa*, Dakar, CODESRIA.
Kieh, G. and Railey, D., 1993, 'Women, Sexual Harassment and Employment Opportunities in Liberia *Liberian Studies Journal*, Vol. 18 No 2 pp. 189-202.
Knauss, P. R., 1992, 'Algerian Women Since Independence' in Entelis and P. C., Naylor (1992).
Knudsen, C. O., 1994, *The Falling Dawadawa Tree: Female Circumcision in Developing Ghana*, Hojberg, Denmark, Intervention Press.
Koso-Thomas, O., 1987, *The Circumcision of Women: A Strategy for Eradication*, London, Zed.
Kurwijila, R., 1990, 'The Role of Appropriate Technology in Reducing Women's Workload in Agricultural Activities in Tanzania' Office of Women in International Development Working Paper 208, Michigan State University.
Kyomuhendo, G. B., 1992, 'The Role of Women in Petty Commodity Production and Commerce: A Case Study of Rural Women in Uganda', CBR, Workshop Paper.
Lazreg, M., 1990, 'Gender and Politics in Algeria: Unravelling the Religious Paradigm', *Signs*, Vol. 15, No 4, pp. 755-780.
Lazreg, M., 1994, *The Eloquence of Silence: Algerian Women in Question*, London and New York Routledge.
Leith-Ross, S., 1939, *African Women: A Study of the Ibo of Nigeria*, London.
Lippert, A., 1992, 'Sahrawi Women in the Liberation Struggle of the Sahrawi People', *Signs*, Vol. 17, No 3, pp. 636-651.
Lue-Mbizvo, C., 1991, 'The Role of Women in Small-Scale Bread-making, Bick Making and Beer Brewing Industries in Rural Zimbabwe' ZERO Regional Network of Environmental Experts no 23.
Mack, B., 1992, 'Harem Domesticity in Kano', Nigeria in K.T. Hansen 1992 ed.
Mackintosh, M., 1989, *Gender, Class and Rural Transition: Agribusiness and the Food Crisis in Senegal*, London, Zed Press.
Macleod, A. E., 1991, *Accomodating Protest: Working Women, the New Veiling and Social Change in Cairo*, New York, Columbia Univ. Press.
Magaia, 1989, *Dumba Nengue: Peasant Tales of Genocide in Mozambique*, London, Karnak House.
Mager, A., 1989, 'Moving the Fence: Gender in the Ciskei and Border Textile Industry, 1945-1986' *Social Dynamics*, Vol. 15, No 2, pp. 46-62.
Mair, L.M., 1986, 'International Review of Women and Development Studies' ISS/UNESCO Workshop, Nov. 19, The Hague, Institute of Social Studies.
Mama, Amina 1996 'Conceptualising Colonial and Contemporary Violence Against African Women' in C. Mohanty and A. Torres ed., Feminist Geneologies, Routledge, New York.

Mama, A., 1996, ed., *Setting an Agenda for Gender and Women's Studies in Nigeria*, Report of Workshop held at British Council, Kaduna, 8-12th January.

Mama, A., 1995a, 'Feminism or Femocracy? State Feminism and Democratisation in Nigeria', *Africa Development*, Vol. XX, No 1, pp. 37-58, Dakar CODESRIA.

Mama, A., 1995b, *Beyond the Masks: Race, Gender and Subjectivity*, London and New York, Routledge.

Mangwat, J. and Abama, E.A., 1993, 'Gender and Access to Education: The Nigerian Situation *AALAE Journal*, Vol. 7, No 2, pp. 33-38.

Mann, K., 1985, *Marrying Well: Marriage, Status and Social Change Among the Educate Elite in Colonial Lagos*, Cambridge African Studies series.

Manuh, 1993, 'Women, the State and Society Under the PNDC' in Gyimah-Boadi (1993).

Manuh, T., 1991a, 'Women and their Organisations During the Convention People's Party Period' in Arhin (1991a).

Manuh, T., 1991b, 'The Status of Research on Women in Ghana', ASA Conference Paper.

Marks, S., 1994, *Divided Sisterhood: Race, Class and Gender in the South African Nursing Profession*, New York/Macmillan, Basingstoke, St Martin's Press.

Marshall, R., 1991, 'Power in the Name of Jesus' *Review of African Political Economy* Publication, Oxford.

Mashinini, E., 1989, *Strikes Have Followed me all my Life*, The Women's Press, London.

Mba, N., 1989, 'Kaba and Khaki: Women and the Militarized State in Nigeria' in Parpart and Staudt (1989).

Mbata, J.N. and Amadi, C.J., 1990, 'The Role of Women in Traditional Agriculture: A Case Study of Women in Food Crop Production in Rivers State', *Nigeria, Ahfad Journal*, Vol. 7, No 1, pp. 32-50.

Mbeo, M.A. and Ooko-Ombaka, O. eds., 1989, *Women and Law in Kenya*, Nairobi, Public Law Institute.

Mbilinyi, M., 1984, 'Women in Development Ideology: The Promotion of Competition and Exploitation' *The African Review*, Vol. 11, No 1.

Mbilinyi, M., 1989, 'This is an Unforgettable Business: Colonial State Intervention in Urban Tanzania' in Parpart and Staudt (1989).

Mbilinyi, M., 1991, *Big Slavery*, Dar Es Salaam University Press.

Mbilinyi, M., 1992, 'Change in Work and Household Relations: The Case of Sugar Cane Plantation Workers', CBR Workshop Paper.

McClintock, A., 1995, 'No Longer in a Future Heaven: Women and Nationalism in South Africa' in *Transition*, 51, pp. 104-123.

McFadden, P., 1992, 'Nationalism and Gender Issues in South Africa', *Journal of Gender Studies*, Vol. 1, No 4, pp. 510-520.

McFarland, J., 1988, 'Review Essay: The Construction of Women and Development Theory' *Review of Canadian Sociology and Anthropology*, Vol. 25, No 2.

Mckintosh, M., 1989, *Gender, Class and Rural Transition: Agribusiness and the Food Crisis in Senegal*, London, Zed Books.

Meagher, K. and Yunusa, M-B., 1993, 'Informalisation and its Discontents: Coping with Structural Adjustment in the Nigerian Urban Informal Sector', unpub research report, Geneva, UNRISD.

Meagher, K., 1991, 'Limits to Labour Absorption: Conceptual and Historical Background to Adjustment in the Nigerian Urban Informal Sector', Discussion Paper 29, Geneva, UNRISD.

Meena, Ruth, 1992, *Gender in Southern Africa: Conceptual and Theoretical Issues*, Harare, SAPES Book.

Meintjes, S., 1990, 'Family and Gender in the Christian Community at Edendale, Natal, in Colonial Times' in Walker (1990 ed.).

Mensah Kuti, R., 1991, 'The Pattern of Women's Work in Ghanaian Industry', Workshop Paper on Women Organising in the Process of Industrialisation, The Netherlands, Institute of Social Studies.

Mernissi, F., 1975, *Beyond the Veil: Male-Female Dynamics in a Modern Muslim Society*, Cambridge, Massachusetts Schenkman.

Mies, M., 1979, 'Towards a Methodology of Women's Studies', The Hague, The Netherlands Institute of Social Studies, Working Paper.

Mies, M., and Reddock, R., 1982 edS., *National Liberation and Women's Liberation*, The Hague Institute of Social Studies.

Mikell, G., and Skinner, E. P., 1989, 'Women and the Early State in West Africa', Michigan State University, Office of Women in International Development, Working Paper 190.

Mirza, S. and Strobel, M. eds., 1989, *Three Swahili Women: Life Histories from Mombasa*, Kenya, Indiana University Press, Bloomington and Indianapolis.

Mitullah, W., 1991, 'Hawking as a Survival Strategy for the Urban Poor in Nairobi: The Case of Women' *Environment and Urbanization*, Vol. 3, No 2, pp. 13-22.

Moghadam, V., 1994a ed., *Gender and National Identity: Women and Politics in Muslim Societies*, London, Zed books.

Moghadam, V., 1994b ed., *Identity Politics and Women: Cultural Reassertions and Feminisms in International Perspective*, Boulder, San Francisco, Oxford, Westview Press.

Mogwe, A., 1994, 'Human Rights in Botswana: Feminism, Oppression and Integration' Alternatives, No 19, pp. 189-193.

Mohanty C., Russo A. and Torres L., 1991, *Third World Women and The Politics of Feminism*, Indiana, Indiana University Press.

Mohanty C. and L. Torres eds., 1996 *Feminist Geneologies*, London New York, Routledge.

Mohanty, C., 1988, 'Under Western Eyes: Feminist Scholarship and Colonial Discourse' *Feminist Review* 30.

Molapo, L., 1991, 'Women's Studies in Lesotho' Paper presented to Conference on 'African Women's Studies', Ohio State University, Nov. 1991.

Moran, N.H., 1990, *Civilised Women: Gender and Prestige in Southeastern Liberia*, Ithaca and London, Cornell University Press.

Morsy, S.A., 1988, 'Fieldwork in My Egyptian Homeland: Towards the Demise of Anthropology's Distinctive-Other Hegemonic Tradition' in Altorki and E. Sohl (1988).

Morsy, S.A., 1991, 'Women and Contemporary Social Transformation in North Africa' in *Women and International Development Annual* 2.

Moser, C., 1989, 'Gender Planning in the Third World: Meeting Practical and Strategic Gender Needs' *World Development*, Vol. 17, No 11.

Mueller, A., 1986, 'The Bureaucratization of Feminist Knowledge: The Case of Women in Development', *Resources for Feminist Research 15*.

Mugo, M., 1994, 'The Woman Artist in Africa Today' *Africa Development*, Vol. XIX, No 1, pp. 49-70.

Mugyenyi, M.R., 1992, *The Impact of Structural Adjustment Programmes on Ugandan Rural Women*, CBR Workshop Paper.

Mukurasi, L., 1991, *Post Abolished: One Woman's Struggle for Employment Rights*, London, Women's Press.

Munachonga, M.L., 1989, 'Women and the State: Zambia's Development Policies and their Impact on Women', in Parpart and Staudt (1989).

Munachonga, M.L., 1991, 'The Status of Women's Studies in Africa: Review of Selected Literature on Women in Zambia', ASA Conference Paper, 23-26 November, St Louis, Missouri.

Musisi, N., 1991, 'Women, "Elite Polygyny", and Buganda State Formation', *Signs*, Vol. 16, No 4, pp. 757-786.

Musisi, N., 1992, 'Colonial and Missionary Education: Women and Domesticity in Uganda, 1900-1945', in Hansen (1992).

Musoke, M., 1992 ed., 'Development of Academic Courses in Gender Studies in Eastern and Southern Africa', Proceedings of Makerere Women's Studies Department/OSSREA, Workshop, Entebbe, Uganda 3-5 Sept.

Muthwa, S., 1994, 'Female Household Headship and Household Survival in Soweto' *Journal Gender Studies*, Vol. 3, No 2, pp. 165-175.

Mwaka, V.M. and Kasente, D., 1991, 'The Status of Women's Studies in Uganda', Ohio State University, Conference on African Women's Studies, 22-26 Nov., Columbus, Ohio.

Naanen, B., 1991, 'Itinerant Gold Mines: Prostitution in the Cross River Basin of Nigeria, 1930-1950' *African Studies Review*, Vol. 34, No 2, pp. 57-79.

Narayan, U., 1989, 'The Project of Feminist Epistemology: Perspectives From a Non-Western Feminist', in Jaggar and Bordo 1989 eds.

National Council for Research/Sudan Family Planning Association, 1989, 'Women's Studies in the Sudan', Workshop Papers.

Nelson, N., 1981, ed., *African Women in the Development Process*, London, Frank Cass and Co.

Ngaiza, M.K. and Koda, B. eds., 1991, *The Unsung Heroines: Women's Life Histories from Tanzania Women*, Dar-es-Salaam, Research and Documentation Project.

Nkebukwa, A.K., 1990, 'Social-cultural factors and their Impact on the Participation of Women in Income-generating Activities: Views from Kwimba District, Mwanza Region' Women's Research and Documentation Project, Dar Es Salaam.

Nzomo, M., 1993, 'The Gender Dimension of Democratization in Kenya: Some International Linkages' *Alternatives*, Vol. 18, pp. 61-73.

Obbo, C., 1989, 'Sexuality and Economic Domination in Uganda' in Yuval-Davis and Anthias (eds.).

Ochwada, Hannington, 1995, 'Gender Analysis: The Stunted Discourse in Kenya's Historiography', *Africa Development*, Vol. XX, n 4, pp. 11-28, Dakar CODESRIA.

Oduyoye M.A. and Kanyoro R.A., 1992 eds., *The Will to Arise: Women, Tradition and the Church in Africa*, New York, Maryknoll.

Ogbomo, O.W., 1993, 'Assertion and Reaction: A Definitive View of Women and Politics in Nigeria' in *Pakistan Statistical Year Book*, Vol. 5, No 1-2, pp. 59-71.

Okine, V., 1993, 'The Survival Strategies of Poor Families in Ghana and the Role of Women Therein' in Okine (1993 ed.).

Okonjo, K., 1983, 'The Dual-sex System in Operation: Igbo Women and Community Politics in Midwestern Nigeria' in Hafkin and Bay (1983 eds.).

Olenja, J.M., 1991, 'Gender and Agricultural Production in Samia Kenya: Strategies and Constraints' *Journal Eastern African Research and Development*, Vol. 21, pp. 81-92.

Orodho, J.A., 1992, 'Women's Work and the Informal Sector in Kenya: A Study of Some Small-Scale Women Enterprises in Mombassa District' *Eastern Africa Social Science Review*, Vol. 8, No 2, pp. 20-49.

Oyekanmi, F. D., 1994, 'Women's Attitude Towards Sexually Transmitted Disease in Nigeria: A Case Study in Blesa in Osun State', *Africa Development*, Vol. XIX, n 2, pp. 147-165, Dakar, CODESRIA.

Oyekanmi, F.D., 1994, 'Women's Attitude Towards Sexually Transmitted Disease in Nigeria: A Case Study in Ilesa in Osun State', *Africa Development*, Vol. XIX, No 2, pp. 147-166.

Pala, A.O., 1977, 'Definitions of Women and Development: An African Perspective', *Signs*, Vol. 3, No 1.

Pankhurst, H., 1992, *Gender Development and Identity: An Ethiopian Study*, London, Zed Books.

Parker, A., Russo, M., Sommer, D. and Yaeger, P. eds., 1992, *Nationalisms and Sexualities*, London and New York, Routledge.

Parpart, J.L. and Staudt K.A., 1989 eds., *Women and the State in Africa*, London, Lynner Rienner, Boulder.

Parpart, J.L., 1989 ed., *Women and Development in Africa: Comparative Perspectives*, U.S.A., Dalhousie University.

Patton, C., 1992, 'From Nation to Family: Containing African Aids' in Parker *et al.* eds.

Paulme, D., 1963 ed., *Women of Tropical Africa*, Berkely Univ. California Press.

Pearce, T.O., 1991, 'Women's Studies in Nigeria: Present Trends', ASA Conference Paper.

Perbi, A., 1992, 'Women in the Government Service in the Pre-Independence and Post-Independence Periods of Ghana's History', *Greenhill Journal of Administration*, Vol. 8, No 1, pp. 66-81.

Pickering H. and Wilkins H.A., 1993, 'Do unmarried women in African towns have to sell sex, or is it a matter of choice? *Health Transition Review*, Vol. 3, pp. 17-27.

Pickering H., Todd J., Pepin J. and Wilkins A., 1992, 'Prostitutes and their Clients: A Gambian Survey' *Social Science and Medicine*, Vol. 34, No 1, pp. 75-88.

Pittin, R., 1995, 'Women, Work and Ideology in a Context of Economic Crisis: A Nigerian Case Study', ISS Working Paper, Sub-series on Women, History and Development: Themes and Issues, No. 11, ISS, The Hague

Prah, K.K., 1991 ed., *Culture, Gender, Science and Technology in Africa*, Harp Windhoek.

Preston-Whyte E. and Nene S., 1991, 'Black Women and the Rural Informal Sector' in E.Preston-Whyte and C. Rogerson eds., (1991).

Preston-Whyte, E. and Rogerson, C. 1991 eds., *South Africa's Informal Economy*, Cape Town, Oxford Univ.

Preston-Whyte, E., 1991, 'Invisible Workers: Domestic Service and the Informal Economy' in E. Preston-Whyte and C. Rogerson eds., (1991).

Rahama, A.A., 1989, 'Women's Studies The Case of Ahfad University', NRC/SFPA, Workshop on Women's Studies in the Sudan.

Ranchord-Nilsson, S., 1992, 'Educating Eve: The Women's Club Movement and Political Consciousness Among Rural African Women in Southern Rhodesia, 1950-1980' in K.T. Hansen ed.

Raseroka, H.K. and Mbambo, B., 1991, 'A Bibliographic Essay of Research on Women in Botswana', ASA Conference paper.

Roberts, H., 1981, *Doing Feminist Research*, London, Routledge.

Rosaldo M.Z. and Lamphere, L., 1974 eds., Women, Culture and Society Stanford University Press, California, Stanford.

Russell, D.E.H., 1990, *Lives of Courage: Women for a New South Africa*, London, Virago.

Sadaawi, N., 1980, *The Hidden Face of Eve*, London, Zed.

Sadler, K., 1991, 'Gender Ambiguity in Primary Source Material: The Case of Southern African Rock Art' UFAHAMU, Vol. XIX, No 2-3, pp. 112-127.

Samater, A.I., 1994 ed., *The Somali Challenge: From Catastrophe to Renewal?*, Lynne Rienner, Boulder

Schmidt, E., 1991, 'Patriarchy, Capitalism and the Colonial State in Zimbabwe' Signs, Vol. 16, No 4, pp. 732-756.

Schmidt, E., 1992, *Peasants, Traders, and Wives: Shona Women in the History of Zimbabwe, 1870-1939*, London, Heinemann Portsmouth/Baobab Harare/James Currey.

Seidman, G.W., 1993, 'No Freedom without the Women: Mobilization and Gender in South Africa, 1970-1992', *Signs*, Vol. 18, No 2, pp. 291-320.

Sen, G. and Grown, C., 1987, 'Development, Crises and Alternative Visions: Third World Women's Perspectives', *Development Alternatives with Women for a New Era*, London, Earthscan.

Sender, J. and Smith S., 1990, Poverty, Class and Gender in Rural Africa: A Tanzanian Case Study, London & New York, Routledge.

Shapiro, D., 1990, 'Farm Size, Household Size and Composition, and Women's Contribution to Agricultural Production: Evidence from Zaire', *Journal Development Studies* Vol. 27, No 1, pp. 1-21.

Sheldon, K., 1990, *To Guarantee the Implementation of Women's Emancipation as Defined by the Frelimo Party: The Women's Organisation in Mozambique*, Michigan State University Office of Women in International Development, Working Paper 206.

Shettima, K.A., 1989, 'Women's Movement and Visions: the Nigeria Labour Congress Women's Wing' in *Africa Development*, Vol. XIV, No 3.

Shukrallah, H., 1994, 'The Impact of the Islamic Movement in Egypt', *Feminist Review 47*.

Silberschmidt, M., 1991, 'Rethinking Men and Gender Relations: An Investigation of Men, Their Changing Roles Within the Household and the Implications for Gender Relations in Kisii District, Kenya', Copenhagen, Centre for Development Research.

Silberschmidt, M., 1992, 'Have Men Become the Weaker Sex? Changing Life Situations in Kisii District, Kenya', *Journal of Modern African Studies* Vol. 30, No 2, pp. 237-253.

Skramstad, H., 1990, 'The Fluid Meanings of Female Circumcision in a Multiethnic Context in Gambia: Distribution of Knowledge and Linkages to Sexuality' *Development Research and Action Programme*, Norway, Michelson Institute.

Snyder, M.C. and Tadesse, M., 1995, *African Women and Development: A History*, London, Witwatersrand University Press, Johannesburg and Zed.

Somali Women's Democratic Organisation, 1989, *Female Circumcision: Strategies to Bring About Change* Proceedings of the International Seminar on Female Circumcision, 13-16 June 1988, Mogadiscio, Rome, Italian Association for Women in Development.

Sorenson, A., 1990, *The Differential Effects on Women of Cash Crop Production: The Case of Small-holder Tea Production in Kenya* Centre for Development Research Project Paper 90.3, Copenhagen.

Sorenson, A., 1992, 'Women's Organisations and the Kipsigis: Change, Variety and Different Participation', *Africa*, Vol. 62, No 4.

Sow, A., 1995, 'L'intérêt de l'analyse du genre dans la relation économique entre la femme rurale et son environnement: le cas de Niadiène en moyenne Casamance', *Africa Development*, Vol. XX, n 4, pp. 29-50, Dakar, CODESRIA.

Stanley L. and Wise S., 1983, *Breaking Out: Feminist Consciousness, Feminist Research*, London, Routledge.

Stanley, L., 1990 ed., Feminist Praxis: Research, Theory and Epistemology in Feminist Sociology, London/New York, Routledge.

Staudt K. and Col J.M., 1991, 'Diversity in East Africa: Cultural Pluralism, Public Policy, and the State' in *Women and International Development Annual 2*.

Staunton, I., 1991 ed., *Mothers of the Revolution*, Harare, Baobab.

Suda, C., 1989, 'Differential Participation of Men and Women in Production and Reproduction in Kakamega District: Implications for Equity' *Journal Developing Societies*, Vol. 5, No 2, pp. 234-44.

Summers, C., 1991, 'Intimate Colonialism: The Imperial Production of Reproduction in Uganda, 1907-1925' in *Signs* 16(4):787-807.

Sweetman, D., 1984, *Women Leaders in African History*, Heinemann, London/Ibadan/Nairobi.

Swilla, I.N.; 1992, 'Gender Inequalities in the Teaching Staff of Boys and Girls Secondary Schools in Tanzania: A Comparative Study', *East African Social Science Review*, Vol. VII, No 2, pp. 51-71.

Taire, A.A., 1992, *Women in Management* Administrative Staff College of Nigeria, Occasional Papers, Badagary.

Tlemcani, R., 1992, 'The Rise of Algerian Women: Cultural Dualism and Multi-party Politics', Journal of Developing Societies, Vol. 8, No 1, pp. 69-81.

Toth, J. 1991, 'Pride, Purdah or Paychecks: What Maintains the Gender Division of Labour in Rural Egypt?', *International Journal Middle East Studies*, Vol. 23, No 2, pp. 213-136.

Tripp, A.M., 1989, 'Women and the Changing Urban Household Economy in Tanzania', *Journal of Modern African Studies*, Vol. 27, No 4, pp. 601-623.

Tsikata, E., 1989, 'Women's Political Organisations 1951-1987' in E. Hansen and K. Ninsin eds., The State, Development and Politics in Ghana, CODESRIA.

Turner, T. and O'Connor, P., 1994, 'Women in the Zambian Civil Service: A Case of Equal Opportunities?', *Public Administration and Development*, Vol. 14, No 1, pp. 79-92.

Turner, T. and Oshare, M. O., 1993, 'Women's Uprisings Against the Nigerian Oil Industry in the 1980s' *Canadian Journal of Development Studies*, Vol. 14, No 3, pp. 330-357.

Uchendu, P.K., 1993, The Role of Nigerian Women in Politics, Fourth Dimension, Enugu.

Uitto, J.I., 1989, 'Fertility and Female Education in Kenya: A Regional Interpretation', *Maapallo* 3: 139-143 University of Helsinki.

UN/ECA, 1989, *African Women in Development: Selected Statements*, by Adebayo Adedeji, Addis Ababa.

UN/ECA, 1990, *African Charter for Popular Participation in Development*, Addis Ababa.

UN/ECA/ACTRW, 1982, 'Directory of National Subregional and Regional Machineries for the Integration of Women in Development in African Countries', Addis Abeba.

Urdang, S., 1979, *Fighting Two Colonialisms: Women in Guinea-Bissau*, New York & London, Monthly Review Press.

Urdang, S., 1989, *And Still They Dance: Women, War and the Struggle for Change in Mozambique*, London, Earthscan.

Vaughan, M., 1981, *Curing their Ills: Colonial Power and African Illness*, Polity Press, Cambridge.

VerEecke, C., 1989, *Cultural Construction of Women's Economic Marginality: The Fulbe of Northeastern Nigeria*, Michigan State University Office of Women in International Development, Working Paper 195.

Von Bulow, D., 1992, 'Bigger than Men? Gender Relations and their Changing Meaning in Kipsigis Society Kenya', *Africa*, Vol. 62, No 4, pp. 523-546.

Walker, C. ed., 1990, *Women and Gender in Southern Africa to 1945*, Cape Town, David Philip.

Walker, C., 1982, *Women and Resistance in South Africa*, London, Onyx Press.

Wallace T. and March C., 1991 eds., *Changing Perceptions: Writings on Gender and Development* U.K., Oxfam.

Warsame A. and Ahmed S., 1985, 'Social and Cultural Aspects of Female Circumcision and Infibulation: A Preliminary Report', unpublished Report of the Women's Research Unit, Somali Academy of Sciences and Arts/SAREC.

White, L., 1990, *The Comforts of Home: Women and Prostitution in Colonial Nairobi*, University of Chicago Press.

Whitehead, A., 1990, 'Food Crisis and Gender Conflict in the African Countryside' in The Food Question: Profits Before People? in H. Bernstein, B. Crow, M. Mackintosh, C. Martins eds., London, Earthscan.

Wilson, A., 1991, *The Challenge Road: Women and the Eritrean Revolution*, London, Earthscan.

Wipper, A., 1972, 'The Roles of African Women: Past, Present and Future' *Canadian Journal of African Studies*, Vol. 6, No 2.

Wipper, A., 1988, 'Reflections on the Past Sixteen Years, 1972-1988 and Future Challenges' *Canadian Journal of African Studies*, Vol. 22, No 3, pp. 409-421.

Yuval Davis, N. and F. Anthias, 1989 eds., *Woman-Nation-State*, Macmillan, London.

Zeleza, T., 1993, *Modern Economic History of Africa*, Dakar, CODESRIA.

Zeleza, T., 1993b, 'Gendering African History: Book Review' *Africa Development*, Vol. XVIII, No 1, pp. 99-117.

Achevé d'imprimer
sur les presses de l'Imprimerie Saint-Paul
Angle rues El Hadj Mbaye Guèye (ex Sandiniéry) / Dr Thèze
B.P. 1301 – DAKAR
Décembre 1996